Guitar Chord Songbook

Irish Songs

ISBN 978-1-4234-6804-2

7777 W. BLUEMOUND RD. P.O. BOX 13819 MILWAUKEE, WI 53213

In Australia Contact:
Hal Leonard Australia Pty. Ltd.
4 Lentara Court
Cheltenham, Victoria, 3192 Australia
Email: ausadmin@halleonard.com.au

Visit Hal Leonard Online at
www.halleonard.com

Contents

Arthur McBride

Traditional Irish Folk Song

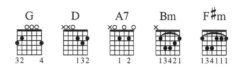

Intro

|G |D |A7 |D |

Verse 1

    D   G   D
I had a first cousin called Arthur Mc - Bride.

     G   D   G   A7
He and I took a stroll down by the sea - side,

   D   Bm   G   D
A seeking good fortune and what might be - tide,

       F#m G A7
'Twas just as the day was a dawn - ing.

    D   G   D
Then after resting we both took a tramp,

   G   D   G   A7
We met Sergeant Harper and Corporal Cramp

    D   Bm   G   D
Be - sides the wee drummer who beat up for camp,

       A7   D
With his rowdydow - dow in the morning.

Verse 2

```
         D                      G           D
He says, "My young fellows, if you will en - list

  G        D           G          A7
A guinea you quickly shall have in your fist.

   D     Bm          G          D
Be - sides a crown for to kick up the dust,

                     F♯m         G      A7
And drink the king's health in the morn - ing."

   D                      G           D
Had we been such fools as to take the ad - vance,

  G        D           G          A7
The wee bitter morning we had run to chance,

             D        Bm        G         D
For you'd think it no scruple to send us to France

             A7          D
Where we would be killed in the morning.
```

The Band Played On

Words by John E. Palmer
Music by Charles B. Ward

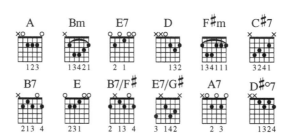

Intro |A |Bm |E7 |A E7 A |

Verse 1

       A   **D**
Matt Casey formed a social club that beat the town for style,

    E7   **A**
And hired for a meeting place a hall.

                                   D
When payday came around each week, they greased the floor with wax,

    E7   **A E7**
And danced with noise and vigor at the ball.

A   **F#m**   **Bm**   **C#7**   **F#m**
  Each Saturday you'd see them, dressed up in Sunday clothes.

    B7   **E B7/F# E7/G#**
Each lad would have his sweetheart by his side.

       A   **D**
When Casey led the first grand march, they all would fall in line

   E7   **A**
Be - hind the man who was their joy and pride.

Chorus 1

    E B7 E7 A
For _____ Casey would waltz with a strawberry blonde,

    E7
And the band played on.

    D
He'd glide 'cross the floor with the girl he adored,

    A
And the band played on.

    E7   A7   D
But his brain was so loaded it nearly ex - ploded,

    Bm
The poor girl would shake with a - larm.

    D$\sharp$°7   A   F$\sharp$m
He'd ne'er leave the girl with the strawberry curls,

    B7 E7   A
And the band played on.

Verse 2

    A   D
Such kissing in the corner and such whisp'ring in the hall,

    E7   A
And telling tales of love behind the stairs.

                 D
As Casey was the favorite and he that ran the ball,

    E7   A E7
Of kissing and lovemaking did his share.

A F$\sharp$m   Bm   C$\sharp$7   F$\sharp$m
  At twelve o'clock ex - actly, they all would fall in line,

    B7   E B7/F$\sharp$ E7/G$\sharp$
Then march down to the dining hall and eat.

    A   D
But Casey would not join them although ev'rything was fine.

    E7   A
But he stayed upstairs and exercised his feet.

Chorus 2   *Repeat Chorus 1*

Verse 3

       A   D
Now when the dance was over and the band played home sweet home,

      E7   A
They played a tune at Casey's own re - quest.

                                  D
He thanked them very kindly for the favors they had shown.

      E7   A E7
Then he'd waltz once with the girl that he loved best.

A   F#m   Bm   C#7   F#m
Most all the friends are married that Casey used to know.

     B7   E B7/F# E7/G#
And Casey, too, has taken him a wife.

     A   D
The blonde he used to waltz and glide with on the ballroom floor,

  E7   A
Is happy Missis Casey now for life.

Chorus 3   *Repeat Chorus 1*

Brennan on the Moor

Traditional

It's a - bout a fierce high - way-man

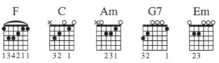

F   C   Am   G7   Em

134211   32 1   231   32 1   23

Intro　　　　|F　　|C　　|F　　|C　　|

Verse 1

           C　　　　　　　　　F　　　C
It's a - bout a fierce highwayman my story I will tell.

                          F　　Am　C
His name was Willy Brennan and in Ireland he did dwell.

                               F　　Am　　C
'Twas up on the King's own mountain he be - gan his wild ca - reer,

F　　　　　　　　　　　　C　　F　　　C
And many a wealthy gentleman be - fore him shook with fear.

Chorus 1

G7　C　　F　　C　　Em
Oh, it's Brennan on the moor, Brennan on the moor.

      F　　　　C　　　　　　　F　　　　　C
Bold, gay and un - daunted stood young Brennan on the moor.

Verse 2

           C　　　　　　　F　　　　C
It was upon the King's highway Old Brennan he sat down.

                      F　　Am　C
He met the mayor of Moorland five miles out - side of town.

                       F　　Am　　C
Now the mayor, he had heard of Brennan and "I think," says he,

F　　　　　　　　　C　　F　　　C
"Your name is Willy Brennan, you must come a - long with me."

Chorus 2   *Repeat Chorus 1*

                 C   F   C

Verse 3   Now Brennan's wife had gone to town pro - visions for to buy,

                               F   Am   C

And when she saw her Willy taken she be - gan to cry.

                                   F   Am   C

Says he, "Hand me that ten penny," and as soon as Willy spoke,

             F   C   F   C

She handed him a blunderbuss from under - neath her cloak.

Chorus 3   *Repeat Chorus 1*

                 C   F   C

Verse 4   Now Brennan got his blunderbuss, my story I'll un - fold.

                               F   Am   C

He caused the mayor to tremble and de - liver up his gold.

                               F   Am   C

Five thousand pounds were offered for his appre - hension there,

             F   C   F   C

But Brennan and the peddler to the mountain did re - pair.

Chorus 4   *Repeat Chorus 1*

                 C   F   C

Verse 5   Now Brennan is an outlaw all on some mountain high.

                             F   Am   C

With infantry and cavalry to take him they did try.

                                   F   Am   C

But he laughed at them and he scorned at them until, it was said,

             F   C   F   C

By a false hearted woman he was cruel - ly be - trayed.

Chorus 5   *Repeat Chorus 1*

Verse 6
      C   F   C
They hung him at the crossroads; in chains he swung and died.

                              F   Am   C
But still they say in the night some do see him ride.

                                F   Am   C
They see him with his blunderbuss in the midnight chill;

      F   C   F   C
A - long, along the King's highway rides Willy Brennan still.

Chorus 6   *Repeat Chorus 1*

Believe Me, If All Those Endearing Young Charms

Words and Music by Thomas Moore

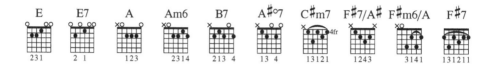

Be - lieve me, if all those en - dear - ing young charms

E	E7	A	Am6	B7	A#°7	C#m7	F#7/A#	F#m6/A	F#7
231	2 1	123	2314	213 4	13 4	13121	1243	3141	131211

Intro |E   E7 |A   Am6 |E   B7 |E |

Verse 1
          E   A   A#°7
Be - lieve me, if all those en - dearing young charms

           E   B7   E B7   E
Which I gaze on so fondly to - day were to change by tomorrow,

      A   A#°7   E   B7   E
And fleet in my arms like fairy gifts fading a - way,

                           C#m7   A   F#7/A#
Thou would'st still be a - dored as this moment thou art

          E   F#m6/A B7 E
Let thy loveliness fade as   it   will.

B7   E   E7   A   F#7
And a - round the dear ruin, each wish of my heart

          E   B7   E
Would en - twine itself verdantly still.

Verse 2

$$E \qquad\qquad A \qquad\qquad A\sharp^{\circ}7$$
It is not while beauty and youth are thine own,

$$E \qquad B7 \qquad E$$
And thy cheeks unpro - faned by a tear,

$$B7 \quad E \qquad\qquad A \qquad A\sharp^{\circ}7$$
That the fervor and faith of a soul can be known,

$$E \qquad B7 \qquad\qquad E$$
To which time will but make thee more dear.

$$C\sharp m7 \quad A \qquad F\sharp 7/A\sharp$$
No, the heart that has truly loved never for - gets

$$E \qquad F\sharp m6/A \;\; B7 \;\; E$$
But as truly loves on to   the   close.

$$B7 \;\; E \qquad E7 \qquad\qquad A \qquad F\sharp 7$$
As a sunflower turns on her god, when he sets,

$$E \qquad B7 \qquad\qquad E$$
The same look which she turn'd when he rose.

Black Velvet Band

Traditional Irish Folk Song

Melody:

Her eyes they shun like _____

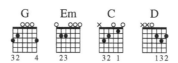

G   Em   C   D

Intro

|G | |Em | |
|C |D |G | |

Chorus 1

      G
Her eyes they shun like diamonds,

              D
You'd think she was queen of the land.

          G   Em
With her hair flung over her shoulders,

        C   D   G
Tied up with a black velvet band.

Verse 1

       G   D
As I ___ went walking down Broadway, not intending to stay very long,

  G   Em   C   D   G
I met with this frolicking damsel as she came tripping a - long.

                                       D
A watch she pulled out all her pocket and slipped it right into me hand.

       G   Em   C   D   G
On the very first day that I met her bad luck to her black velvet band.

Chorus 2 *Repeat Chorus 1*

Verse 2
```
            G                                              D
'Fore judge and jury next morning both of us did ap - pear
      G           Em        C        D        G
A gentleman claimed his jewelry and the case a - gainst us was clear.
                                              D
Seven long years transportation right on down to Van Diemen's land,
      G                          Em        C        D        G
Far a - way from my friends and com - panions to follow the black velvet band.
```

Chorus 3 *Repeat Chorus 1*

Chorus 4 *Repeat Chorus 1*

Come Back to Erin

Irish Folksong

Melody:

Come back to Er - in, Ma - vour - neen, Ma - vour - neen.

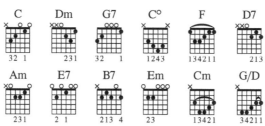

C   Dm   G7   C°   F   D7

Am   E7   B7   Em   Cm   G/D

Intro | C   Dm | C G7 C |

Verse 1

      C   C°   G7   C° C
Come back to Er - in, Ma - vourneen, Ma - vour - neen.

                  F   D7   G7
Come back, a - roon, to the land of my birth.

      C   C°   G7   C° C
Come with the sham - rocks and springtime, Ma - vour - neen,

      Am   D7   G7   C
And its Kil - larney shall ring with our mirth.

Bridge 1

      Am   E7   Am
Sure when we lent ye to beautiful England,

      B7   Em   Am Em B7   E7
Little we thought of the lone winter days.

      Am   E7   Am
Little we thought of the hush of the starshine

      Cm   G/D   D7   G7
Over the mountain, the bluffs and the brays!

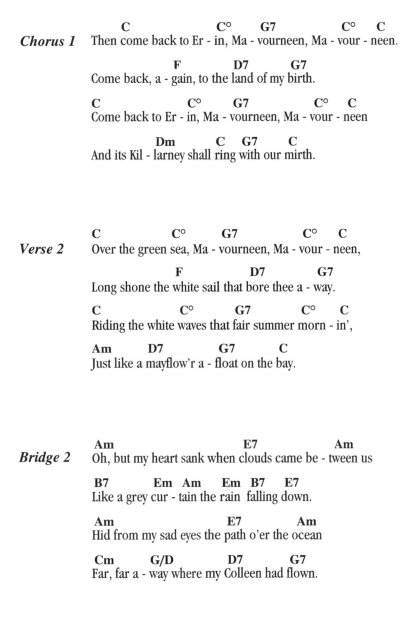

Chorus 1

      C   C°   G7   C°   C
Then come back to Er - in, Ma - vourneen, Ma - vour - neen.

                F   D7   G7
Come back, a - gain, to the land of my birth.

  C   C°   G7   C°   C
Come back to Er - in, Ma - vourneen, Ma - vour - neen

             Dm   C G7   C
And its Kil - larney shall ring with our mirth.

Verse 2

  C   C°   G7   C°   C
Over the green sea, Ma - vourneen, Ma - vour - neen,

                F   D7   G7
Long shone the white sail that bore thee a - way.

  C   C°   G7   C°   C
Riding the white waves that fair summer morn - in',

  Am   D7   G7   C
Just like a mayflow'r a - float on the bay.

Bridge 2

  Am   E7   Am
Oh, but my heart sank when clouds came be - tween us

  B7   Em Am   Em B7   E7
Like a grey cur - tain the rain falling down.

  Am   E7   Am
Hid from my sad eyes the path o'er the ocean

  Cm   G/D   D7   G7
Far, far a - way where my Colleen had flown.

Chorus 2   *Repeat Chorus 1*

Verse 3

     C   C°   G7   C°   C
Oh, may the an - gels, oh, walkin' and sleep - in'

                       F   D7   G7
Watch o'er my bird in the land far a - way.

     C   C°   G7   C°   C
And it's my prayers will con - sign to their keep - in'

     Am   D7   G7   C
Care o' my jewel by night and by day.

Bridge 3

     Am   E7   Am
When by the fireside I watch the bright embers,

     B7   Em Am Em B7   E7
Then all my heart flies to Eng - land and thee,

     Am   E7   Am
Cravin' to know if my darlin' re - members

     Cm   G/D   D7   G7
Or if her thoughts may be crossin' to me.

Chorus 3   *Repeat Chorus 1*

Girl I Left Behind Me

Traditional Irish

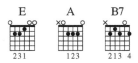

Intro |E |A |B7 |E |

Verse 1

        E
I'm lonesome since I coss'd the hill, and o'er the moor and valley.
              A   **B7**   **E**
Such heavenly thoughts my heart do fill since parting with my Sally.
                                      E
I seek no more the fine and gay, for each does but remind me
  E   **A**   **B7**   **E**   **B7**
How swift the hours did pass away with the girl I left be - hind me.

Verse 2

  E
Oh, ne'er shall I forget the night the stars were bright above me,
              A   **B7**   **E**
And gently lent their silvery light when first she vow'd she loved me.
                                B7
But now I'm bound to Brighton Camp, kind heav'n may favor find me,
  E   **A**   **B7**   **E**
And send me safely back again to the girl I left be - hind me.

Danny Boy

Words by Frederick Edward Weatherly
Traditional Irish Folk Melody

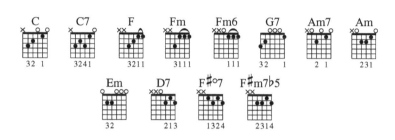

Verse 1

           C   C7   F
Oh, Danny Boy, the pipes, the pipes are calling,

      Fm   C   Fm6 G7
From glen to glen, and down the mountain-side.___

              C   C7 F
The summer's gone, and all the roses falling.

      Fm   C   G7   C
It's you, it's you must go and I must bide.

                   F   G7   Am7
But come ye back when summer's in the meadow,

         Am   F   Em   D7 G7
Or when the valley's hush'd and white with snow.__

         C   F   F#°7 C Am F#m7b5
'Tis I'll be there in sunshine or in shad-ow,_____

    Fm6 C   Am7 F   G7   C
Oh, Danny Boy, oh Danny Boy, I love you so!

Verse 2

       C   C7   F
But if he come, when all the flow'rs are dying,

  Fm C   Fm6
And I am dead, as dead I well may be,

           C   C7 F
Ye'll come and find the place where I am lying,

  Fm   C   G7   C
And kneel and say an Ave there for me;

           F   G7   Am7
And I shall hear, tho' soft your tread a-bove me,

    Am   F   Em   D7 G7
And all my dreams will warm and sweeter be.___

        C   F   F#°7   C   Am F#m7♭5
If you will not fail to tell me that you love me,_____

  Fm6 C   Am7   F   G7   C
Then I shall sleep in peace un-til you come to me!

Easy and Slow

Traditional Irish Folk Song

Intro |C |Em |G7 |C |

Verse 1

      C   **Dm**   **Am**   **Em**
'Twas down by Christ - church that I first met with Annie.

  C   **Am** **Dm** **G7**
A neat little girl and not a bit shy.

    C   **Dm**   **Am**   **Em**
She told me her father who came from Dun - gannon

    C   **Am**   **Dm**   **C**
Would take her back home in the sweet bye and bye.

Chorus 1

   Am   **Em**
And what's it to any man whether or no.

Am   **Dm**   **G7**
Whether I'm easy or whether I'm true.

   Am   **Em**
As she lifted her petticoat easy and slow,

   C   **Am**   **Dm** **G7 C**
And I rolled up my sleeves for to buckle her shoe.

Verse 2

```
        C        Dm   Am       Em
All a - long Thomas Street, down to the Liffey,

        C        Am        Dm       G7
The sunshine was gone and be evening grew dark.

        C        Dm       Am   Em
A - long in Kings - bridge and be - god in a jiffy;

        C        Am        Dm       C
Me arms were a - round her be - yond in the park.
```

Chorus 2   *Repeat Chorus 1*

Verse 3

```
        C    Dm       Am       Em
From city or county the girl she's a jewel,

        C        Am        Dm       G7
And well made for gripping the most of them are.

        C    Dm    Am   Em
But any young man he is really a fool

        C        Am        Dm   C
If he tries at the first time to go a bit far.
```

Chorus 3   *Repeat Chorus 1*

Verse 4

```
        C        Dm   Am       Em
Now if you should go to the town of Dun - gannon,

        C        Am        Dm   G7
You search till your eyes they are weary or blind.

        C    Dm    Am   Em
Be you lying or walking or sittin' or runnin'

        C        Am        Dm   C
A lassie like Annie you never will find.
```

Chorus 4   *Repeat Chorus 1*

The Foggy Dew

Traditional Irish Folk Song

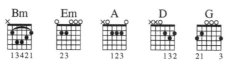

Verse 1

Bm   Em   A
Over the hills I went one day;

Bm Em Bm
A lovely maid I spied.

                          Em   A
With her coal-black hair and her mantle so green,

Bm Em Bm
An image to per-ceive.

   D   G   D   A
Says I, "Dear girl, will you be my bride?"

     Bm   Em F#m Bm
And she lifted her eyes of__ blue.

                      Em   A
She smiled and said, "Young man, I'm to wed;

   Bm   Em Bm
I'm to meet him in the foggy dew."

GUITAR CHORD SONGBOOK

Verse 2

Bm　　　　　**Em**　　**A**
Over the hills I went one morn,

　Bm　　**Em Bm**
A singing I did go.

　　　　　　　　　　Em　　　**A**
Met this lovely maid with her coal-black hair,

　　　Bm　　　**Em**　　　**Bm**
And she answered soft and low.

　　　D　　　　**G**　　　　**D**　　**A**
Said she, "Young man, I'll be your bride,

　Bm　　　　**Em**　**F#m Bm**
If I know that you'll be___ true."

　　　　　　　　Em　**A**
Oh, in my arms, all of her charms

　　　Bm　　　　**Em**　**Bm**
Were casted in the foggy dew.

Harrigan

Words and Music by
George M. Cohan

Who   is   the man   who will spend   or   will e - ven lend?

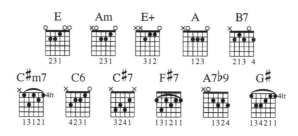

E   Am   E+   A   B7

C#m7   C6   C#7   F#7   A7♭9   G#

Intro

|E Am E Am |E E+ A E | B7 |E   A   E |

Verse 1

E   Am E   Am   E   E+   A E
Who is the man who will spend or will even lend?

B7   E   C#m7 C6 B7
Harrigan,   that's me!

E   Am E   Am   E   E+   A   E
Who is your friend, when you find that you need a friend?

B7   E A
Harrigan,   that's me!

E
For I'm just as proud of my name, you see,

B7   E   B7
As an emperor, czar or a king could be.

E   Am E   Am   E   E+   A   E
Who is the man helps a man ev'ry time he can?

B7   E   A E
Harrigan,   that's me!

GUITAR CHORD SONGBOOK

Chorus 1

E C#7 F#7   B7   E   B7
H - A - double R-I-G-A-N spells Harrigan.

E   B7
Proud of all the Irish blood that's in me.

                        E
"Devil" a man can say a word a - gin' me.

E C#7 F#7   B7   A7b9 G#
H - A - double R-I-G-A-N, you   see,

N.C. E   Am E   Am E E+   A   E
Is a   name that a shame never has been con - nected with,

         B7   E A E
Harrigan,   that's me!

Chorus 2   *Repeat Chorus 1*

Verse 2

E Am E Am E E+ A   E
Who is the man never stood for a 'gada - bout?

        B7   E C#m7 C6 B7
Harrigan,   that's me!

E Am E Am   E E+ A   E
Who is the man that the town's simply mad a - bout?

        B7   E A
Harrigan,   that's me!

E
   Thy ladies and babies are fond of me,

B7 E   B7
I'm fond of them, too, in re - turn you see.

E Am E Am   E E+ A   E
Who is the gent that's de - serv - ing a monu - ment?

        B7   E A E
Harrigan,   that's me!

Chorus 3   *Repeat Chorus 1*

I Once Loved a Lass

Traditional Irish Folk Song

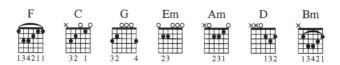

F   C   G   Em   Am   D   Bm

134211   32 1   32 4   23   231   132   13421

Intro |F |C |G   C |G |

Verse 1
```
        G                  Em     C          Am
I once loved a lass ___ and I loved her so well
        G      C        F        D
That I hated all others that spoke of her ill.
        G          C     G        Bm
But now she's re - warded me well for my love
            F        C       G   C
For she's gone to be wed with an - other.
```


Verse 2
```
    G                  Em      C                Am
When I saw my love ___ walk through the church door
        G           C        F       D
With groom and bride maidens they made a fine show.
        G           C      G       Bm
And I followed them in with my heart full of woe
    F          C      G   C
For now she is wed to an - other.
```

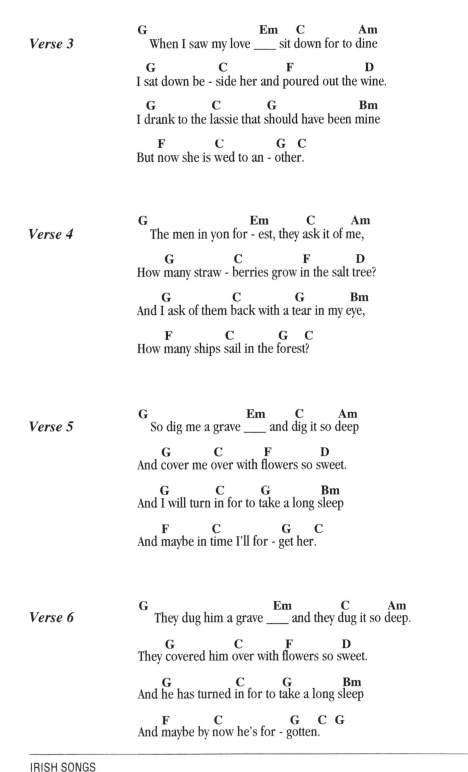

Verse 3

    G   Em   C   Am
    When I saw my love ____ sit down for to dine

    G   C   F   D
    I sat down be - side her and poured out the wine.

    G   C   G   Bm
    I drank to the lassie that should have been mine

     F   C   G C
    But now she is wed to an - other.

Verse 4

    G   Em   C   Am
    The men in yon for - est, they ask it of me,

     G   C   F   D
    How many straw - berries grow in the salt tree?

     G   C   G   Bm
    And I ask of them back with a tear in my eye,

     F   C   G C
    How many ships sail in the forest?

Verse 5

    G   Em   C   Am
    So dig me a grave ____ and dig it so deep

     G   C   F   D
    And cover me over with flowers so sweet.

     G   C   G   Bm
    And I will turn in for to take a long sleep

     F   C   G   C
    And maybe in time I'll for - get her.

Verse 6

    G   Em   C   Am
    They dug him a grave ____ and they dug it so deep.

     G   C   F   D
    They covered him over with flowers so sweet.

     G   C   G   Bm
    And he has turned in for to take a long sleep

     F   C   G   C G
    And maybe by now he's for - gotten.

I'll Take You Home Again, Kathleen

Words and Music by
Thomas Westendorf

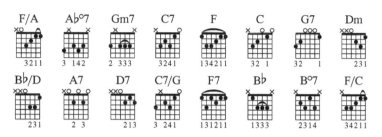

Intro |F/A A♭°7 |Gm7 C7 |

Verse 1

            F   C7   A♭°7   F/A
I'll take you home a - gain, Kath - leen,

            C7   F
A - cross the ocean wild and wide,

    C7 F   C7   A♭°7 F/A
To where your heart has ever   been

            C   G7   C7
Since first you were my bonny bride.

        Gm7 C7   F
The roses all have left your cheek,

        C7   F
I've watched them fade away and die.

            Dm   B♭/D   A7
Your voice is sad when - e'er you speak

    D7   G7   C7
And tears bedim your loving eyes.

Chorus 1

    F   C7/G A♭°7   F/A
Oh, I will take you back, Kath - leen,

    C7   F
To where your heart will feel no pain.

C7 F   F7   B♭
And when the fields are fresh and green

B°7 F/C   C7   F
I'll   take you to your home, Kath - leen.

Verse 2

    F   C7   A♭°7 F/A
To that dear home be - yond the sea

    C7   F
My Kathleen shall again re - turn.

C7   F   C7   A♭°7 F/A
  And when thy old friends welcome thee

    C   G7   C7
Thy loving heart will cease to yearn.

    Gm7   C7   F
Where laughs the little silver stream

    C7   F
Be - side your mother's humble cot

    Dm   B♭/D A7
And brightest rays of sunshine gleam,

    G7   C7
There all your grief will be for - got.

Chorus 2   *Repeat Chorus 1*

I'll Tell Me Ma

Traditional Irish Folk Song

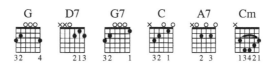

G	D7	G7	C	A7	Cm

Intro |G   D7 |G |

Verse 1

        G
I'll tell me ma, when I go home,

    D7   **G**
The boys won't leave the girls alone.

They pull my hair, they stole my comb,

    D7   **G**
And that's alright till I go home.

      G7   **C** **D7**
She is handsome, she is pretty,

G   **A7**   **D7**
She's the belle of Belfast city.

G **G7**   **C**   **Cm**
She is courtin', one, two, three.

G   **D7** **G**
Please won't you tell me who is she?

Verse 2

          G
Now Albert Mooney says he loves her,

D7   **G**
All the boys are fighting for her.

They rap at the door and ring the bell,

      D7   **G**
Saying, "Oh, my true love, are you well?"

    G7   **C**   **D7**
Out she comes, as white as snow,

G   **A7**   **D7**
Rings on her fingers, bells on her toes.

G   **G7**   **C**   **Cm**
Old Jenny Murphy says she'll die,

G   **D7**   **G**
If she doesn't get the fellow with the roving eye.

Verse 3

          G
Let the wind and the rain and the hail blow high

    D7   **G**
And the snow come shov'ling from the sky.

She's as nice as apple pie,

     D7   **G**
And she'll get her own lad by and by.

    G7 **C**   **D7**
When she gets a lad of her own,

G   **A7**   **D7**
She won't tell her ma when she gets home.

G   **G7**   **C**   **Cm**
Let them all come as they will,

G   **D7** **G**
But it's Albert Mooney she loves still.

I'm a Rover and Seldom Sober

Traditional Irish Folk Song

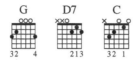

Intro |G D7 |G |

Chorus 1

        G   C   G
I'm a rover and seldom so - ber,

            D7
I'm a rover o' high de - gree.

        G   D7 G
It's when I'm drinking I'm always thinking

         D7   G
How to gain my love's compa - ny.

Verse 1

        G   C   G
Though the night be as dark as dun - geon,

            D7
No' a star to be seen a - bove,

        G   D7 G
I will be guided with - out a stumble

         D7   G
Into the arms o' my ain true love.

Chorus 2   *Repeat Chorus 1*

Verse 2

       G   **C**   **G**
He steppit up to her bedroom win - dow,

                D7
Kneelin' gently upon a stone,

      G   **D7**   **G**
He rappit at her bedroom window,

              D7 **G**
"Darlin', dear, do you lie a - lone?"

Chorus 3   *Repeat Chorus 1*

Verse 3

       G   **C**   **G**
She raised her heid on her snawhite pil - low,

             D7
Wi' her arms aboot her breast,

      G   **D7**   **G**
"Wha' is that at my bedroom window,

           D7   **G**
Disturbin' me at my lang night's rest?"

Chorus 4   *Repeat Chorus 1*

Verse 4

       G   **C**   **G**
"It's only me, your ain true lov - er,

               D7
Open the door and let me in,

      G   **D7** **G**
For I hae come on a lang journey

           D7   **G**
And I'm near drenched to the skin."

Chorus 5   *Repeat Chorus 1*

Verse 5

     G   C   G
She opened the door wi' the greatest pleas - ure,

                                    D7
She opened the door and she let him in.

            G   D7   G
They baith shook hands and embraced each other,

              D7   G
Until the mornin' they lay as one.

Chorus 6   *Repeat Chorus 1*

Verse 6

     G   C   G
The cocks were crawin', the birds were whist - lin',

                             D7
The burns they ran free abune the brae.

           G   D7   G
"Remember, lass, I'm a ploughman laddie

              D7   G
And the faimer I must o - bey."

Chorus 7   *Repeat Chorus 1*

Verse 7

     G   C   G
"Noo, my lass, I must gang and leave thee,

                             D7
And though the hills they are high a - bove,

           G   D7   G
I will climb them wi' great pleasure

              D7   G
Since I been in the arms o' my love."

Jug of Punch

Ulster Folk Song

Melody:

'Twas ver - y ear - ly in the month of June

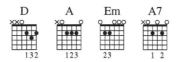

Intro |D | | | |

Verse 1

          D
'Twas very early in the month of June

   A   **D**
I was sitting with my glass and spoon.

               Em
A small bird sat on an ivy bunch,

      A   **D**
And the song he sang was "The Jug of Punch."

A7   **D**
Too-rah - loo-rah-loo, too-rah-loo-rah lay.

       A7   **D**
Too-rah - loo-rah-loo, too-rah - loo-rah lay.

               Em
A small bird sat on an ivy bunch,

      A   **D**
And the song he sang was "The Jug of Punch."

Verse 2

                              D
What more di - version can a man desire,

           A   D
Than to court a girl by a neat turf fire?

                     Em
A Kerry pippin and the crack and crunch,

     A   D
And on the table a jug of punch.

A7   D
Too-rah - loo-rah-loo, too-rah-loo-rah lay.

        A7   D
Too-rah - loo-rah-loo, too-rah - loo-rah lay.

                     Em
A Kerry pippin and the crack and crunch,

     A   D
And on the table a jug of punch.

Verse 3

                    D
All ye mortal Lords drink your nectar wine,

           A   D
And the noble folks drink their claret fine.

                    Em
I'll give them all the grapes in the bunch

     A   D
For a jolly pull at the jug of punch.

A7   D
Too-rah - loo-rah-loo, too-rah-loo-rah lay.

        A7   D
Too-rah - loo-rah-loo, too-rah - loo-rah lay.

                    Em
I'll give them all the grapes in the bunch

     A   D
For a jolly pull at the jug of punch.

Verse 4

         D
Oh, but when I'm dead and in my grave,

     A   **D**
No costly tombstone will I crave.

             Em
Just lay me down in my native peat

     A   **D**
With a jug of punch at my head and feet.

A7   **D**
Too-rah - loo-rah-loo, too-rah-loo-rah lay.

       A7   **D**
Too-rah - loo-rah-loo, too-rah - loo-rah lay.

             Em
Just lay me down in my native peat

     A   **D**   **A7 D**
With a jug of punch at my head and feet.

Ireland Must Be Heaven, For My Mother Came from There

Words by Joseph McCarthy and Howard Johnson
Music by Fred Fisher

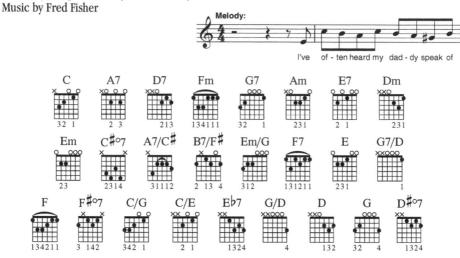

Intro　　　　|C　　A7 |D7　Fm　G7　C |

Verse 1

　　　　　　　Am　　　　　E7　　　　　　A7　　　　　　　Dm
I've often heard my daddy speak of Ireland's lakes and dells.

　　　　　　Am　　　　　　　　　　　　Em　　Am　Em
The place must be like heaven, if it's half like what he tells.

C#°7　　Dm　G7　　　C　　　　　A7/C#　G7　　　　　　C
There's roses fair and shamrocks there and laughing waters flow.

　　　　　Em　　　B7/F#　Em/G
I have never seen that　　Isle of Green,

　　　　　B7/F#　　F7　　E　　G7/D
But there's one thing sure, I know.

Chorus 1

     C   E7 F F$\sharp^{\circ}$7 C/G

Ireland must be heaven, for an angel came from there.

 G7 C   F C/E E$\flat$7 G/D Am D G

I never knew a living soul one half as sweet or fair.

     C   A7   D   G7

For her eyes are like the starlight and the white clouds match her hair.

 D$\sharp^{\circ}$7 C   A7   D7 Fm G7 C

Sure Ireland must be heaven, for my mother came from there.

Verse 2

    Am   E7   A7   Dm

I've pictured in my fondest dreams old Ireland's vales and rills.

    Am   Em Am Em

I see a stairway to the sky, formed by her verdant hills.

 C$\sharp^{\circ}$7 Dm   G7   C A7/C$\sharp$ G7   C

Each wave that's in the ocean blue just loves to hug the shore.

   Em   B7/F$\sharp$ Em/G   B7/F$\sharp$ F7   E G7/D

So, if Ireland is - n't   heaven, then sure, it must be right next door.

Chorus 2   *Repeat Chorus 1*

The Irish Rover

Traditional Irish Folk Song

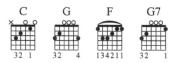

In the year of our Lord, eigh-teen hun-dred and six,

C	G	F	G7

Intro |C |G   C |

Verse 1

         C   F
In the year of our Lord, eighteen hundred and six,

         C   G
We set sail from the Cole Quay of Cork.

          C   F
We were sailing away with a cargo of bricks,

          C   G7   C
For the grand City Hall in New York.

                                 G
We'd an elegant craft, it was rigged fore and aft,

       C   G
And how the tradewinds drove her.

         C   F
She had twenty-three masts and she stool sev'ral blasts,

          C   G   C
And they called her the Irish Rov - er.

GUITAR CHORD SONGBOOK

Verse 2

                   C   F
There was Barney McGee from the banks of the Lee.

                   C   G
There was Hogan from County Ty - rone.

                   C   F
There was Johnny McGurk, who was scared stiff of work,

               C   G7   C
And a chap from Westmeath named Ma - lone.

                                        G
There was Slugger O'Toole, who was drunk as a rule,

           C   G
And fighting Bill Tracy from Dover.

                   C   F
And your man, Mick McCann, from the banks of the Bann,

           C   G   C
Was the skipper on the Irish Ro - ver.

Isn't It Grand Boys

Traditional Irish Folk Song

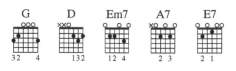

G   D   Em7   A7   E7

Intro

|G | |D | |
|Em7 |A7 |D |A7 |

Verse 1

A7   D   G
Look at the coffin with golden handles.

        D   E7   A7
Isn't it grand, boys, to be bloody-well dead?

Chorus 1

                    D   G   D
Let's not have a sniffle, let's have a bloody good cry.

        G   D
And always remember, the longer you live,

        Em7   A7   D
The sooner you'll bloody-well die.

Verse 2

A7   D   G
Look at the flowers all bloody-well withered.

        D   E7   A7
Isn't it grand, boys, to be bloody-well dead?

Chorus 2   *Repeat Chorus 1*

Verse 3	A7 D G Look at the mourners, all bloody-great hypocrites. D E7 D Isn't it grand, boys, to be bloody-well dead?
Chorus 3	*Repeat Chorus 1*
Verse 4	A7 D G Look at the preacher, bloody-nice fellow. D E7 A7 Isn't it grand, boys, to be bloody-well dead?
Chorus 4	*Repeat Chorus 1*
Verse 5	A7 D G Look at the widow, bloody-great female. D E7 D Isn't it grand, boys, it be bloody-well dead.
Chorus 5	*Repeat Chorus 1*

Kerry Dance

By J. L. Molloy

Oh, the days of the Ker - ry danc - ing!

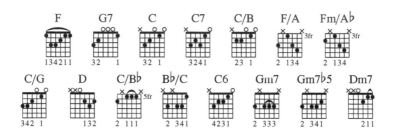

Intro |F | | | |

Chorus 1

F
Oh, the days of the Kerry dancing!

                G7   **C**
Oh, the ring of the piper's tune!

F
Oh, for one of those hours of gladness,

               C7   **F**
Gone, alas, like our youth, too soon.

GUITAR CHORD SONGBOOK

Verse

C   C/B   F/A   Fm/A♭
When the boys be - gan to gather

C/G   D   G7
In the glen of a summer night,

C   C/B♭ F/A   Fm/A♭
And the Kerry   pipers tuning

C/G   G7   C
Made us long with wild de - light.

B♭/C   C6
Oh, to think of it! Oh, to dream of it

Gm7   Gm7♭5   C7
Fills my heart with tears.

Chorus 2

F
Oh, the days of the Kerry dancing!

             G7   C
Oh, the ring of the piper's tune!

F
Oh, for one of those hours of gladness,

       Dm7   Gm7 C7   F
Gone, a - las, like our youth, ____ too soon.

Killarney

Words and Music by
Michael W. Balfe

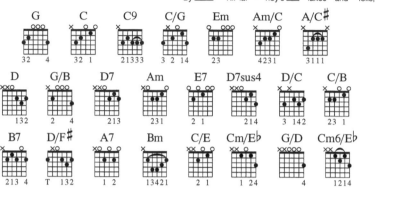

Intro |G   C |G   C9 |

Verse 1

G   C   G   C/G G
By Kil - larney's lakes and fells,

         Em   Am/C A/C♯ D
Em'rald isles and wind - ing   bays,

G   C   G   C/G G
Mountain paths and wood - land dells,

         G/B C   D7   G
Mem'ry ev   -   er fondly strays.

Em   Am   G   C G
Bounteous nature loves all lands.

E7   Am   Em Am D7sus4 D7
Beauty wanders ev - 'ry - where,

C   D/C G/B C/B Am B7 Em
Foot - prints leaves on   man - y   strands,

D   D/F♯ G D   A7 D
But her home is sure- ly   there.

G/B   C   G/B C   G   D
An - gels fold their wings and rest

Am   Bm D7 G/B   C
In that E - den of the West.

G   C G/B   C G C
Beau - ty's home, Kil - lar - ney!

C/E Cm/E♭ G/D   Cm6/E♭ D7 G
Ev   -   er   fair, Kil - lar   -   ney!

Verse 2

G   C   G   C/G   G
Innis - fallen's ru - ined shrine

          Em   Am/C   A/C♯   D
May sug - gest a pass - ing   sigh,

G   C   G   C/G   G
But man's faith can ne'er de -   cline

            G/B   C   D7   G
Such God's won - ders floating by.

Em   Am   G   C   G
Castle Lough and Glen - a - Bay,

E7   Am   Em   D7sus4   D7
Mountain's Tore and Ea - gle's Nest.

C   D/C   G/B   C/B Am B7   Em
Still at   Muck - ross you   must pray,

D   D/F♯   G   D   A7   D
Though the monks are now at   rest.

G/B   C   G/B   C   G   D
An - gels won - der not that man

Am   Bm   D7   G/B   C
There would fain pro - long life's span.

G   C   G/B C   G   C
Beau - ty's home, Kil - lar - ney!

C/E   Cm/E♭   G/D   Cm6/E♭   D7   G
Ev -   er   fair, Kil - lar   -   ney!

Verse 3

G   C   G   C/G   G
No place else can charm the   eye

          Em   Am/C   A/C♯   D
With such bright and var - ied   tints.

G   C   G   C/G   G
Ev'ry rock you pass   by,

           G/B   C   D7   G
Verdure 'broid - ers or be - sprints.

Em   Am   G   C   G
Virgin there the green grass grows.

E7   Am   Em   A7   D7sus4   D7
Ev'ry morn springs na - tal   day.

C   D/C G/B C/B Am   B7 Em
Bright hued dair - ies daft   the snows.
D   D/F# G D   A7 D
Smiling win - ters frown a - way.
G/B   C   G/B C G   D
An - gels, of - ten pausing there,
Am   Bm D7 G/B   C
Doubt if E - den were more fair.
G   C G/B C G   C
Beau - ty's home, Kil - lar - ney!
C/E Cm/Eb   G/D   Cm6/Eb D7   G
Ev -   er   fair, Kil - lar   -   ney!

Verse 4

G   C   G C/G G
Music there for ech - o   dwells,
         Em   Am/C A/C# D
Make each sound a har - mo - ny.
G   C   G   C/G G
Many - voiced, the chor - us   swells
     G/B C D7   G
'Til it faints in ecsta - sy.
Em   Am   G C G
With the charmfull tints be - low,
E7   Am   Em A7 D7sus4 D7
Seems the Heav'n a - bove to   vie.
C D/C G/B C/B Am B7 Em
All rich   col - ors   that we know
D   D/F# G   D A7 D
Tinge the cloud wreaths in that sky.
G/B C G/B C G   D
Wings of an - gels so might shine,
Am   Bm D7 G/B   C
Glancing back soft light di - vine.
G   C G/B C G   C
Beau - ty's home, Kil - lar - ney!
C/E Cm/Eb   G/D   Am7 D7   G
Ev -   er   fair, Kil - lar   -   ney!

Mary's a Grand Old Name

Words and Music by
George M. Cohan

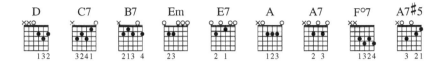

Intro |D C7 B7 | Em |E7 A |D |

                        D   B7 E7   A7   D

Verse   For it is Mar - y,   Mar - y, plain as any name can be.

                             F°7 A7 Em A7   A7#5 D
But with proprie - ty so - ci - e - ty will say Ma - rie.

                         B7 E7   A7   D
But it was Mar - y, Mary , long before the fashions came.

                         C7   B7   Em
And there is some - thing there that sounds so fair,

                         E7   A7 D
It's a grand old name.

MacNamara's Band

Words by John J. Stamford
Music by Shamus O'Connor

Melody:

Oh! Me name is Mac - Na - ma - ra,

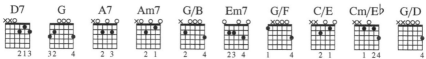

| D7 | G | A7 | Am7 | G/B | Em7 | G/F | C/E | Cm/E♭ | G/D |

Verse 1

   D7   G   A7   D7   G
Oh! Me name is MacNamara, I'm the leader of the band.

     Am7   D7   G/B   Em7   A7   D7
Al - though we're few in number, we're the finest in the land.

    G   A7 D7   G
We play at wakes and weddings and at ev'ry fancy ball.

G/F C/E   Cm/E♭ G/D Em7 A7   D7   G
 And when we play at   funer - als we play the march from Saul.

Chorus 1

   D7   G
Oh! The drums go bang, and the cymbols clang

            D7   G
And the horns they blaze a - way.

     Am7 D7   G/B   Em7
Mc - Carthy pumps the old ba - zoon

     A7   D7
While I the pipes do play.

    G
And Hennessey Tennessee tootles the flute,

        D7   G
And the music is something grand.

G/F C/E Cm/E♭ G/D Em7
 A credit to old   Ire - land

  A7   D7   G
Is MacNa - mara's band.

Verse 2

    G   A7 D7   G
Now we are rehearsin' for a very swell af - fair,

    Am7 D7   G/B   Em7 A7   D7
The annual cele - bration, all the gentry will be there.

        G   A7   D7 G
When Gen'ral Grant to Ireland came he took me by the hand,

G/F   C/E Cm/E♭ G/D   Em7 A7   D7   G
Says he, "I never   saw the likes of MacNa - mara's band."

Chorus 2   *Repeat Chorus 1*

Molly Malone (Cockles & Mussels)

Irish Folksong

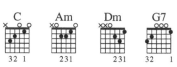

C	Am	Dm	G7
32 1	2 3 1	2 3 1	32 1

Verse 1

      C   Am
In Dublin's fair city

      Dm   G7
Where girls are so pretty,

    C   Am   G7
I first set my eyes on sweet Molly Malone,

      C   Am
As she pushed her wheel-barrow

    Dm   G7
Thro' streets broad and narrow

      C   Am   Dm   C
Crying, "Cockles and mussels, a-live, alive, oh!

Chorus 1

       Am
"Alive, alive, oh!

   Dm   G7
A-live, alive, oh!"

      C   Am
Crying, "Cockles and mussels,

   Dm   C
A-live, alive, oh!"

Verse 2

  C Am
She was a fish-monger,

  Dm   G7
But sure 'twas no wonder,

  C Am G7
For so were her father and mother before.

    C   Am
And they each wheeled their barrow

  Dm   G7
Thro' streets broad and narrow

    C Am Dm C
Crying, "Cockles and mussels, a-live, alive, oh!

Chorus 2 Repeat Chorus 1

Verse 3

  C Am
She died of a fever,

  Dm   G7
And no one could save her,

  C Am G7
And that was the end of sweet Molly Malone.

   C   Am
But her ghost wheels her barrow

  Dm   G7
Thro' streets broad and narrow

    C Am Dm C
Crying, "Cockles and mussels, a-live, alive, oh!

Chorus 3 Repeat Chorus 1

Mother Machree

Words by Rida Johnson Young
Music by Chauncey Olcott and Ernest R. Ball

Melody:

There's a spot in my heart which no col-leen may own.

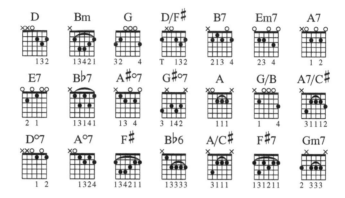

Intro |D   Bm |G D |D/F♯   B7 |Em7   A7 |

Verse 1

          D   Bm   G   D

There's a spot in my heart which no col - leen may own.

          G   D   E7   B♭7 A7

There's a depth in my soul never sounded or   known.

          D   Bm   A♯°7 G   G♯°7

There's a place in my mem'ry, my life,   that you fill.

     D/F♯   E7   B♭7 A

No other can take it. No one ev - er   will.

Chorus 1

    G/B A7/C♯ D   D°7 D   A7 A°7
    Sure I   love the   dear sil - ver

    A7 D   D°7 A7 D
    That shines in   your hair.

              G   F♯   G   D
    And the brow that's all fur - rowed

    Bm E7   B♭6 A G/B
    And wrinkled with care.

    A/C♯ D   D°7 D   A7 A°7
    I   kiss the   dear fin - gers

    A7 D/F♯ G   F♯7 Bm
    So toil - worn for   me.

    F♯ F♯7 G   D   Gm7   D
    Oh, God   bless you and keep you, Mother Ma - chree!

Verse 2

           D   Bm   G   D
    Ev'ry sorrow or care in the dear days gone by

                     G   D   E7   B♭7 A7
    Was made bright by the light of the smile in your eye.

           D   Bm   A♯°7 G   G♯°7
    Like a candle that's set in a win - dow at night,

                      D/F♯   E7   B♭7 A
    Your fond love has cheered me and guided me   right.

Chorus 2   *Repeat Chorus 1*

Mrs. Murphy's Chowder

Irish Folksong

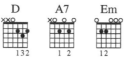

Won't you bring back,   won't you bring back

D   A7   Em

Intro |D | | |A7 D |

Verse 1

           D   A7
Won't you bring back, won't you bring back Missus Murphy's chowder?

                              D
It was tuneful, ev'ry spoonful made you yodel louder.

          A7   D   A7
After dinner, Uncle Ben used to fill his fountain pen

D   A7   D
From a plate of Missus Murphy's chow - der.

Chorus 1

          D
It had ice cream, cold cream, benzene, gasoline,

                   A7
Soup beans, string beans floating all around.

D
Sponge cake, beef steak, mistake, stomach ache,

                 A7
Cream puffs, earmuffs, many to be found.

Em
Silk hats, doormats, bed slats, Democrats,

A7
Coco bells, doorbells beckon you to dine.

D
Meatballs, fish balls, mothballs, cannonballs,

            A7   D
Come on in, the chowder's fine!

Verse 2

            D   A7
Won't you bring back, won't you bring back Missus Murphy's chowder?

                                            D
From each helping, you'll be yelping for a headache powder.

            A7   D   A7
And if they had it where you are, you might find an Austin car

D   A7   D
In a plate of Missus Murphy's chow - der.

Chorus 2   *Repeat Chorus 1*

Verse 3

            D   A7
Won't you bring back, won't you bring back Missus Murphy's chowder?

                                           D
You can pack it, you can stack it all around the larder.

            A7   D   A7
The plumber died the other day, they embalmed him right away

D   A7   D
In a bowl of Missus Murphy's chow - der.

Chorus 3   *Repeat Chorus 1*

Muirsheen Durkin

Traditional Irish Folk Song

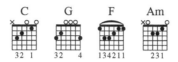

Intro |C |G | |C |

Verse 1

          C   G   F   C
In the days I went a - courtin' I was never tired re - sortin'

        Am   G   F G C
To the ale house or a playhouse or many's a house be - sides.

    Am   G   F   C
I told me brother Seamus I was going to be right famous

        Am   G   F G   C
And be - fore I would re - turn again I'd roam the whole world wide.

Chorus 1

C   G   F C
Goodbye Muirsheen Durkin, sure I'm sick and tired of workin',

    Am   G   F G C
No more I'll dig the praties, no longer I'll be fooled.

    Am   G   F   C
For sure's me name is Carney, I'll be off to Cali - fornee

        Am   G   F   C   G
And in - stead of digging praties I'll be digging lumps of gold.

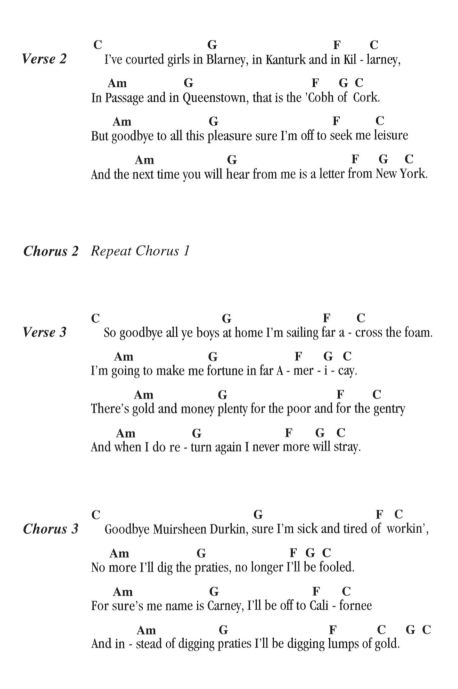

Verse 2

    C   G   F   C
I've courted girls in Blarney, in Kanturk and in Kil - larney,

Am   G   F   G C
In Passage and in Queenstown, that is the 'Cobh of Cork.

Am   G   F   C
But goodbye to all this pleasure sure I'm off to seek me leisure

Am   G   F   G   C
And the next time you will hear from me is a letter from New York.

Chorus 2   *Repeat Chorus 1*

Verse 3

    C   G   F   C
So goodbye all ye boys at home I'm sailing far a - cross the foam.

Am   G   F   G C
I'm going to make me fortune in far A - mer - i - cay.

Am   G   F   C
There's gold and money plenty for the poor and for the gentry

Am   G   F   G C
And when I do re - turn again I never more will stray.

Chorus 3

    C   G   F C
Goodbye Muirsheen Durkin, sure I'm sick and tired of workin',

Am   G   F G C
No more I'll dig the praties, no longer I'll be fooled.

Am   G   F   C
For sure's me name is Carney, I'll be off to Cali - fornee

Am   G   F   C   G C
And in - stead of digging praties I'll be digging lumps of gold.

My Wild Irish Rose

Words and Music by Chauncey Olcott

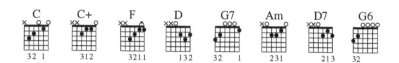

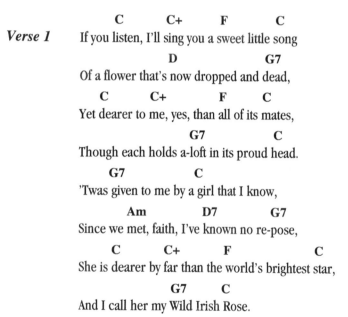

Verse 1

      C   C+   F   C
If you listen, I'll sing you a sweet little song
             D   G7
Of a flower that's now dropped and dead,
     C   C+   F   C
Yet dearer to me, yes, than all of its mates,
              G7   C
Though each holds a-loft in its proud head.
     G7   C
'Twas given to me by a girl that I know,
        Am   D7   G7
Since we met, faith, I've known no re-pose,
      C   C+   F   C
She is dearer by far than the world's brightest star,
         G7   C
And I call her my Wild Irish Rose.

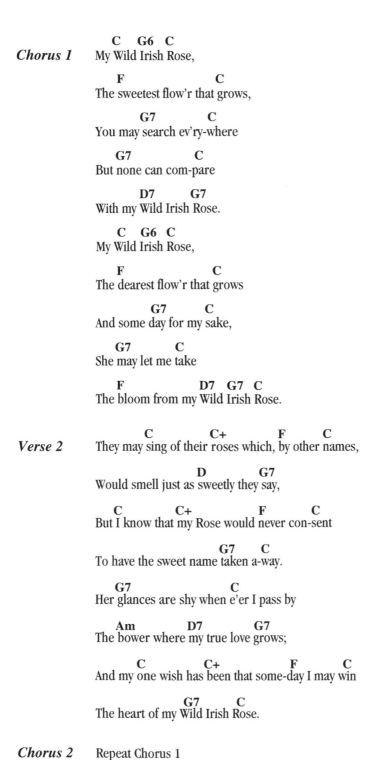

Chorus 1

     C G6 C
My Wild Irish Rose,

       F   C
The sweetest flow'r that grows,

       G7   C
You may search ev'ry-where

       G7   C
But none can com-pare

         D7   G7
With my Wild Irish Rose.

     C G6 C
My Wild Irish Rose,

       F   C
The dearest flow'r that grows

          G7   C
And some day for my sake,

       G7   C
She may let me take

       F   D7 G7 C
The bloom from my Wild Irish Rose.

Verse 2

         C   C+   F   C
They may sing of their roses which, by other names,

             D   G7
Would smell just as sweetly they say,

     C   C+   F   C
But I know that my Rose would never con-sent

         G7   C
To have the sweet name taken a-way.

   G7   C
Her glances are shy when e'er I pass by

    Am   D7   G7
The bower where my true love grows;

      C   C+   F   C
And my one wish has been that some-day I may win

       G7   C
The heart of my Wild Irish Rose.

Chorus 2   Repeat Chorus 1

A Nation Once Again

Words and Music by
Thomas Davis

When _ boy-hood's _ fire _ was _ in my blood

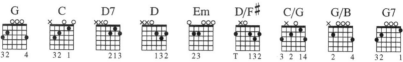

G   C   D7   D   Em   D/F#   C/G   G/B   G7

Intro

|G C G D7 |

Verse 1

G D7   G   D   Em C G C G
When boy - hood's fire was in my blood

D/F# G   D
I read of an - cient free - men,

G   D   Em   C   G   C/G G
For Greece and Rome who brave - ly   stood

C   G   D7 G
Three-hun - dred men and three men.

D7   G/B
And there I prayed I   yet might see

D7 G7 C   G7 C
Our fet - ters rent in   twain,

D7 G   D   Em C G   C
And Ire - land, long a prov - ince,

G   C   G   D7 G
Be a na - tion once a - gain.

Chorus 1

G   C/G   G   C/G   G
A nation once a - gain, a nation once a - gain.

D7/F# G   D   Em C G   C   G
May   Ire - land, long a prov - ince, be

C   G   D7 G
A na - tion once a - gain.

Verse 2

     G   D   Em   C   G C
And from that time, through wild - est woe,

G   G   D/F♯ G D
That hope has shown a   far light.

G   D   Em C   G   C   G
Nor could love's brightest sum - mer glow

         C G   D7 G
Outshine that sol - emn starlight.

               D7 G/B
It seemed to watch a - bove my head

   D7 G7 C   G7 C
In for - um, field and fane.

D7 G C Em   C   G   C   G
It's an - gel voice sang 'round my bed,

        C   G   D7 G
"A na - tion once a - gain."

Chorus 2   *Repeat Chorus 1*

Verse 3

G D   Em C   G   C   G
It whis - pered too, that "Free - dom's Ark"

         D/F♯   G   D
And service high and ho - ly,

        G D   Em C G   C/G G
Would be pro - faned by feel - ings   dark

      C   G   D7   G
And pas - sions vain or lowly.

                D7 G/B
For freedom comes from God's right hand,

    D7   G7 C   G7 C
And needs a   God - ly   train,

D7 G   D   Em C   G   C   G
And right - eous men must make our land

      C   G   D7 G
A na - tion once a - gain.

Chorus 3   *Repeat Chorus 1*

Verse 4

```
G D Em C          G   C G
So  as I    grew from boy to  man,

      D/F#  G        D
I bent me at      the bid - ding.

   G    D Em C   G   C G
My spir - it of   each self - ish plan

         C   G   D7  G
And cruel pas - sion rid - ding.

              D7   G/B
For thus I hoped some day to aid

   D7 G7  C    G7 C
Oh! Can such hope be  vain

D7  G  D  Em   C G  C G
When my dear coun - try shall be made

      C   G   D7  G
A na - tion once a  -  gain?
```

Chorus 4   *Repeat Chorus 1*

The Patriot Game

Traditional Irish Folk Song

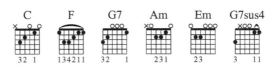

Intro

| C | F | C | |
| G7 | C | | |

Verse 1

>   C   F   C   G7   C
> Come all you young reb - els and list while I sing.
>
>   G7   C Am Em   G7sus4
> For love of one's land is a terrible thing.
>
>   G7   C Am   Em   F
> It banishes fear with the speed of a flame.
>
>   C   F C G7   C
> And makes us all part of the patriot game.

Verse 2

>   C   F C G7   C
> My name is O' - Han - lon, I'm just gone six - teen.
>
>   G7   C   Am Em   G7sus4
> My home is in Mon - aghan, there I was weaned.
>
>   G7   C Am   Em   F
> I was taught all my life cruel England to blame.
>
>   C   F C G7   C
> And so I'm a part of the patriot game.

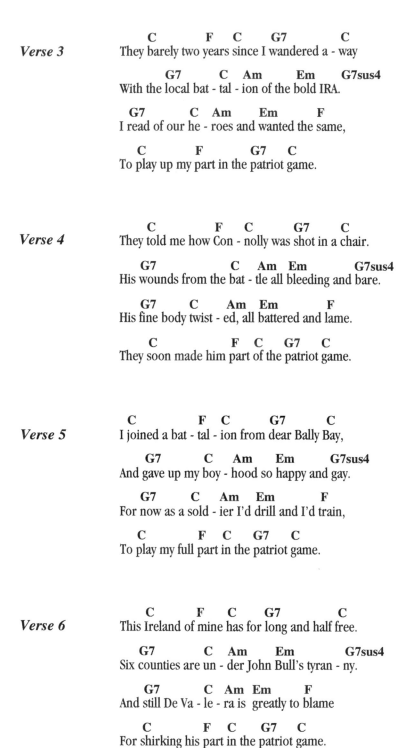

Verse 3

      C   F   C   G7   C
They barely two years since I wandered a - way

         G7   C Am   Em   G7sus4
With the local bat - tal - ion of the bold IRA.

G7   C Am   Em   F
I read of our he - roes and wanted the same,

     C   F   G7   C
To play up my part in the patriot game.

Verse 4

      C   F   C   G7   C
They told me how Con - nolly was shot in a chair.

     G7   C Am Em   G7sus4
His wounds from the bat - tle all bleeding and bare.

     G7   C   Am Em   F
His fine body twist - ed, all battered and lame.

      C   F   C   G7   C
They soon made him part of the patriot game.

Verse 5

C   F   C   G7   C
I joined a bat - tal - ion from dear Bally Bay,

     G7   C   Am   Em   G7sus4
And gave up my boy - hood so happy and gay.

     G7   C   Am   Em   F
For now as a sold - ier I'd drill and I'd train,

     C   F   C   G7   C
To play my full part in the patriot game.

Verse 6

      C   F   C   G7   C
This Ireland of mine has for long and half free.

     G7   C Am   Em   G7sus4
Six counties are un - der John Bull's tyran - ny.

     G7   C Am Em   F
And still De Va - le - ra is greatly to blame

     C   F   C   G7   C
For shirking his part in the patriot game.

Verse 7

```
        C          F  C  G7          C
I don't mind a bit if I shoot down po - lice.

         G7       C  Am  Em       G7sus4
They're lackeys for war never guardians of peace.

         G7      C   Am   Em      F
But yet at de - sert - ers I'm never let aim,

          C        F   C    G7   C
Those rebels who sold out the patriot game.
```

Verse 8

```
         C     F  C     G7    C
And now as I lie with my body all holes

   G7          C   Am    Em        G7sus4
I think of those trai - tors who bargained and sold.

    G7     C   Am  Em        F
I'm sorry my rif - le has not done the same

          C        F   C    G7   C
For the quisling who sold out the patriot game.
```

The Parting Glass

Irish Folksong

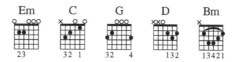

Intro
|Em   C |G   D |Em Bm |Em D Em |

Verse 1

    Em C   G   D
O, all the money e'er I had,

   G   Bm   D
I spent it in good compa - ny,

   Em C   G   D   G
And all the harm I've ever done a - las,

   Bm   Em
It was to none but me.

     G   Em   Bm
And all I've done for want of wit

    Am   Em Bm   D
To mem'ry now I can't re - call

    Em C   G   D
So fill to me the parting glass,

     G   Bm   Em C Em
Good - night and joy be with you all.

Verse 2

    Em C   G   D
O, all the comrades e'er I had,

      G   Bm D
They're sorry for my go - ing a - way.

    Em C   G   D
And all the sweethearts e'er I had,

      G   Bm   Em
They'd wish me one more day to stay.

      G   Em Bm
But since it falls un - to my lot,

   Am Em   Bm D
I gently rise and softly call,

    Em   C   G   D
That I should go and you should not.

      G   Bm   Em C Em
Good - night and joy be with you all.

Verse 3

    Em C   G   D
If I had money e - nough to spend,

    G   Bm D
And leisure time to sit a - while,

    Em C   G   D
There is a fair maid in this town

    G   Bm   Em
That sorely has my heart beguiled.

    G   Em Bm
Her rosy cheeks and ruby lips,

  Am   Em   Bm   D
I own she has my heart in thrall.

    Em C   G   D
Then fill to me the parting glass,

    G   Bm   Em C Em
Good - night and joy be with you all.

Peggy O'Neil

Words and Music by Harry Pease,
Ed. G. Nelson and Gilbert Dodge

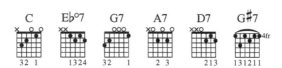

Intro |C | | | |

Verse

      C   Eb°7 G7
If her eyes are blue as skies, that's Peggy O' - Neil.

                                          C
If she's smiling all the while, that's Peggy O' - Neil.

      Eb°7   G7
If she walks like a sly little rogue,

C   Eb°7   G7
If she talks with a cute little brogue,

C   A7   D7
Sweet person - ality, full of rascality,

      G#7 G7   C
That's   Peggy O' - Neil.

The Rising of the Moon

Traditional Irish Folk Song

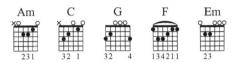

Am   C   G   F   Em

231   32 1   32 4   134211   23

Intro |Am | C |Am   G |Am |

Verse 1	**Am** **C** Oh, then tell me, Sean O' - Farrell,
	Am G F Em Tell me why you hurry so?
	Am **C** Hush, a while, just hush and listen,
	Em **G Am** And his cheeks were all a - glow.
	G **Em** I bear orders from the Captain,
	Am C F G Get you ready quick and soon,
	Am **C** For the pikes must be to - gether
	F C G Am G Am At the rising of the moon!

Verse 2

Am   C
Oh, then tell me, Sean O' - Farrell,

Am   G   F   Em
Where the gathering is to be?

Am   C
In the old spot by the river,

        Em   G   Am
Right well known to you and me.

             G   Em
One word more for signal token

Am   C   F   G
Whistle up the marching tune,

Am   C
With your pike upon your shoulder,

F   C   G   Am G Am
By the rising of the moon!

Verse 3

Am   C
Out from many a mudwall cabin

Am   G   F   Em
Eyes were watching through the night.

Am   C
Many a manly breast was throbbing

       Em   G   Am
For the blessed warning light.

             G   Em
Murmurs passed a - long the valley,

Am   C   F   G
Like the banshee's lonely croon,

Am   C
And a thousand blades were flashing

F   C   G   Am G Am
At the rising of the moon!

Verse 4

Am   C
There beside the singing river

Am G F Em
That dark mass of men were seen.

Am   C
Far above the shining weapons

     Em G Am
Hung their own im - mortal green.

     G Em
Death to ev'ry foe and traitor,

Am C F   G
Forward strike the marching tune,

Am   C
And, hurrah, my boys for freedom,

F   C G Am G Am
'Tis the rising of the moon.

Red Is the Rose

Irish Folk Song

Melody:

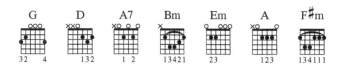

Come o - ver the hills

G   D   A7   Bm   Em   A   F♯m

Intro |G |D |A7 |D |

Verse 1

       D   Bm   Em   G
Come over the hills my bonny Irish lass,

D   Bm   G A
Come over the hills to your dar - ling.

G   F♯m   G Em   G
You choose the rose, love, and I will make the vow,

       D   G   A7 D A7
And I'll be your true love for - ev - er

Chorus 1

       D   Bm   Em   G
Red is the rose that by yonder garden grows.

D   Bm   G A
Fair is the lily of the val - ley.

G   F♯m   G Em   G
Clear is the water that flows from the Boyne.

       D   G   A7 D A7
But my love is fairer than an - y.

GUITAR CHORD SONGBOOK

Verse 2

    D   **Bm**   **Em**   **G**
'Twas down by Kil - larney's green woodlands that girl stayed.

D   **Bm**   **G** **A**
The moon and the stars they were shin - ing.

 G   **F♯m**   **G** **Em** **G**
The moon shone its beams through her locks of golden hair.

    D   **G**   **A7 D A7**
She swore she would love me for - ev - er.

Chorus 2   *Repeat Chorus 1*

Verse 3

    D   **Bm** **Em**   **G**
 But time passes on and my darling girl is gone.

D   **Bm**   **G** **A**
She's gone and met with an - oth - er.

 G **F♯m**   **G**   **Em**   **G**
I'm full of re - gret but my heart will ne'er for - get

   D   **G**   **A7 D A7**
That once she was truly my lov - er.

Chorus 3   *Repeat Chorus 1*

Verse 4

    D   **Bm** **Em** **G**
It's not for the parting that my sister pains,

D   **Bm** **G** **A**
Not for the grief of my moth - er.

 G **F♯m** **G** **Em G**
It's all for the loss of my bonny Irish lass

   D **G**   **A7 D A7**
That my heart is broken for - ev - er.

Chorus 4   *Repeat Chorus 1*

The Rose of Tralee

Words by C. Mordaunt Spencer
Music by Charles W. Glover

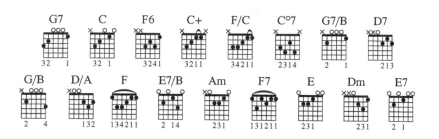

Intro

|G7 |C   F6 |C   G7 |C |

Verse 1

        C   C+ F/C   C°7   C
The pale moon was rising a - bove the green moun - tain.

     G7/B   C   D7   G/B D/A
The sun was de - clining be - neath the blue sea

G7   C   C+ F/C   C°7 C
When I strayed with my love to the pure crystal foun - tain

   G7/B   C   F C G7   C
That stands in the beauty - ful vale of Tra - lee.

Chorus 1

          C   E7/B Am   F   F6 F7 E
She was lovely ___ and fair as the rose of the summer,

  Am   Dm Am   F7   E7 Am Dm
Yet 'twas not her   beauty a - lone that won me.

G7 C   C+ F/C   C°7   C
Oh, no! 'Twas the truth in her eye ever dawn - ing

   G7/B   C   F6   C G7   C
That made me love Mary, ___ the rose of Tra - lee.

|G7 |C   F6 |C   G7 |C |

```
              C                    C+  F/C      C°7    C
Verse 2    The cool shades of evening their mantle was spread - ing,

              G7/B   C          D7        G/B  D/A
           And Mary, all smiling, was list'ning to me.

           G7  C                    C+  F/C       C°7   C
           The moon through the valley her pale rays was shed - ding

              G7/B     C      F  C  G7     C
           When I won the heart of the rose of Tra - lee.
```

```
              C    E7/B    Am      F    F6 F7 E
Chorus 2   Though lovely ____ and fair as the rose of   the summer,

              Am    Dm  Am      F7      E7  Am Dm7
           Yet 'twas not her    beauty a - lone that won me.

           G7  C                    C+  F/C     C°7     C
           Oh, no! 'Twas the truth in her  eye ever dawn - ing

              G7/B        C    F6     C   G7     C
           That made me love Mary, ____ the rose of Tra - lee.

           |G7       |C    F6 |C    G7     |C        ||
```

Sweet Rosie O'Grady

Words and Music by Maude Nugent

Just clown a-round the cor-ner of the

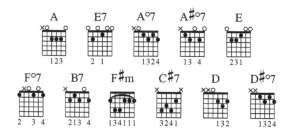

Intro |A   E7 |A A°7 A A#°7 |E   F°7 |B7   E7 |

Verse 1

    A   E7   A   A°7 A
Just down around the corner of the street where I re - side

A#°7   E   F°7   B7   E7
   There lives the cutest little girl that I have ever spied.

    A   E7   A   A°7 A
Her name is Rose O' - Grady and I don't mind telling you

A#°7   E   B7   E7
   That she's the sweetest little Rose the garden ever grew.

Chorus 1

A   E7   A   E7 A E7   A
Sweet Rosie O' - Gra - dy, my dear little Rose,

F#m   C#7 F#m B7   E7
She's my stead - y   lady, most ev'ryone knows.

A E7   A   E7 A D   C#7
And when we are mar - ried, how happy we'll be.

D   D#°7   A F#m B7   E7   A E7
I love sweet Rosie O' - Gra - dy and Rosie O' - Grady loves me.

Verse 2

A		E7		A		A°7 A

I never shall for - get the day she promised to be mine,

A#°7 E   F°7   B7   E7

    As we sat telling love tales in the golden summer - time.

    A   E7   A   A°7   A

'Twas on her finger that I placed a small en - gagement ring

A#°7   E   B7   E7

    While in the trees the little birds this song they seemed to sing.

Chorus 2

A   E7   A   E7 A E7   A

Sweet Rosie O' - Gra - dy, my dear little Rose,

F#m   C#7 F#m B7   E7

She's my stead - y   lady, most ev'ryone knows.

A E7   A   E7 A   D   C#7

And when we are mar - ried, how happy we'll be.

D   D#°7   A   F#m B7   E7   A

I love sweet Rosie O' - Gra - dy and Rosie O' - Grady loves me.

Too-Ra-Loo-Ra-Loo-Ral
(That's an Irish Lullaby)

Words and Music by
James R. Shannon

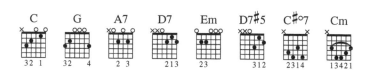

Intro |C | G |A7   D7 |G |

Verse 1

     G   Em   G
Over in Killarney, many years a - go

D7 G   A7   D7
   Me mither sang a song to me in tones so sweet and low.

         G   Em   G
Just a simple little ditty, in her good ould Irish way,

             C   G   A7   D7 D7#5
And I'd give the world if she could sing that song to me this day.

Chorus 1

     G   C   C#°7
Too-ra-loo-ra-loo-ral, too-ra-loo - ra - li,

     G   C   G   A7   D7 D7#5
Too-ra - loo-ra - loo-ral, hush now don't you cry!

     G   C   C#°7
Too-ra-loo-ra-loo-ral, too-ra-loo-ra - li,

     G   C   G   D7   A7   Cm   G
Too-ra - loo-ra - loo-ral, that's an Irish lulla - by.

Verse 2

```
        G                    Em        G
Oft, in dreams, I wander to that cot a - gain.

D7 G                         A7          D7
   I feel her arms a huggin' me as when she held me then.

        G                    Em        G
And I hear her voice a hummin' to me as in days of yore

        C                G        A7        D7  D7♯5
When she used to rock me fast a - sleep out - side the cabin door.
```

Chorus 2

```
G                   C          C♯○7
Too-ra-loo-ra-loo-ral, too-ra-loo - ra-li,

G     C    G    A7           D7  D7♯5
Too-ra - loo-ra - loo-ral, hush now don't you cry!

G                   C          C♯○7
Too-ra-loo-ra-loo-ral, too-ra-loo-ra - li,

G     C    G              A7 C  D7  G
Too-ra - loo-ra - loo-ral, that's an Irish lull - a  - by.
```

Water Is Wide

Traditional

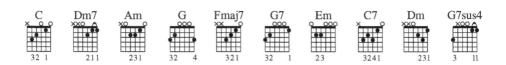

C   Dm7   Am   G   Fmaj7   G7   Em   C7   Dm   G7sus4

Verse 1

                 C   Dm7   C
The water is wide, I cannot get over,

          Am G   Fmaj7   Dm7 G7
And neither have I__ wings to fly._____

        Em   C7   Fmaj7 Dm
Give me a boat____ that can carry two,_____

      G7sus4 G7   C
And both shall row,_____ my love and I.

Verse 2

            C   Dm7   C
I put my hand into some soft bush,

          Am   G Fmaj7 Dm7   G7
Thinking the sweet-est flower to find.___

        Em   C7   Fmaj7 Dm
The thorn, it stuck___ me to the bone,_____

    G7sus4 G7   C
And oh, I left_____ that flower a-lone.

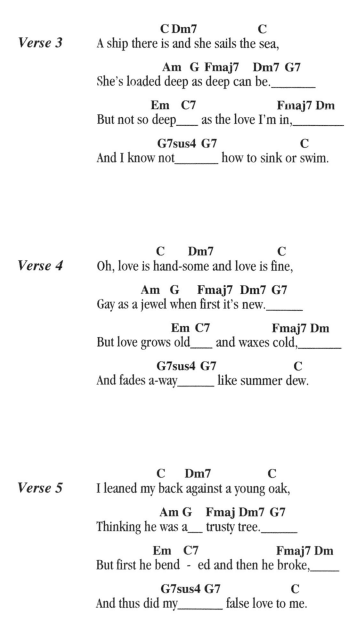

Verse 3
     C Dm7   **C**
A ship there is and she sails the sea,

       Am G Fmaj7   Dm7 G7
She's loaded deep as deep can be._____

       Em   C7   **Fmaj7 Dm**
But not so deep____ as the love I'm in,_____

      G7sus4 G7   **C**
And I know not_____ how to sink or swim.

Verse 4
     C **Dm7**   **C**
Oh, love is hand-some and love is fine,

       Am G **Fmaj7 Dm7 G7**
Gay as a jewel when first it's new._____

       Em C7   **Fmaj7 Dm**
But love grows old____ and waxes cold,_____

      G7sus4 G7   **C**
And fades a-way_____ like summer dew.

Verse 5
     C **Dm7**   **C**
I leaned my back against a young oak,

       Am G **Fmaj Dm7 G7**
Thinking he was a__ trusty tree._____

       Em   C7   **Fmaj7 Dm**
But first he bend - ed and then he broke,____

      G7sus4 G7   **C**
And thus did my_____ false love to me.

The Wearing of the Green

Eighteenth Century Irish Folksong

Oh — Pad-dy dear, and did you hear the

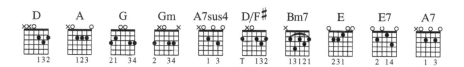

Intro |D | | | |

Verse 1

       D   **A**
Oh, Paddy dear, and did you hear the news that's going 'round?

      G   **D**   **G**   **Gm D**
The shamrock is for - bid by law to grow on Irish ground.

                              A
Saint Patrick's Day no more to keep, his color can't be seen,

G   **D**   **A**   **A7sus4** **D**
For there's a bloody law agin' the wearing of the   green.

D/F# **G**   **D**
I   met with Napper Tandy and he took me by the hand,

D/F# **G**   **D/F#**   **Bm7**   **E** **E7**   **A**
And he said, "How's poor old Ire - land and how does she stand?

A7   **D**   **A**
She's the most distressful country that ever you have seen.

         G   **D**   **A**   **A7sus4** **D**
They're hanging men and women there for wearing of the   green."

Verse 2

      D   A
Then since the color we must wear is England's cruel red,

      G   D   G   Gm   D
Sure Ireland's sons will ne'er forget the blood that they have shed.

                                    A
You may take the shamrock from your hat and cast it on the sod,

      G   D   A   A7sus4 D
But 'twill take root and flourish still, though under - foot it's trod.

D/F♯   G   D
When the law can stop the blades of grass from growing as they grow,

D/F♯ G   D/F♯   Bm7   E   E7   A
And   when the leaves in summer - time their verdure dare not show,

A7 D   A
Then I will change the color that I wear in my corbeen.

      G   D   A   A7sus4 D
But till that day, please God, I'll stick to wearing of the   green!

Verse 3

      D   A
But, if at last our color should be torn from Ireland's heart,

      G   D   G   Gm   D
Her sons, with shame and sorrow, from the dear old soil will part.

                              A
I've heard whispers of a country that lies far beyond the sea,

      G   D   A   A7sus4   D
Where rich and poor stand equal in the light of freedom's day.

D/F♯ G   D
Oh,   Erin, must we leave you, driven by the tyrant's hand?

D/F♯   G   D/F♯   Bm7 E   E7   A
Must we ask a mother's welcome from a strange, but happier land?

A7   D   A
Where the cruel cross of England's thraldom never shall be seen,

      G   D   A   A7sus4 D
And where, thank God, we'll live and die still wearing of the   green!

When Irish Eyes Are Smiling

Words by Chauncey Olcott and George Graff, Jr.
Music by Ernest R. Ball

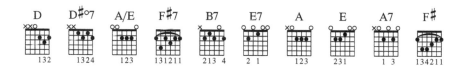

Intro

|D |D#°7 |A/E |F#7 |
|B7 |E7 |A | |

Verse 1

             A
There's a tear in your eye, and I'm wondering why,

                            E7
For it never should be there at all.

A   E7   A   F#7
  With such pow'r in your smile, sure a stone you'd be - guile,

           B7   E
So there's never a teardrop should fall.

E7   A
  When your sweet lilting laughter's like some fairy song,

                A7   D
And your eyes twinkle bright as can be,

           B7   E
You should laugh all the while and all other times, while,

           B7   E
And now smile a smile for me.

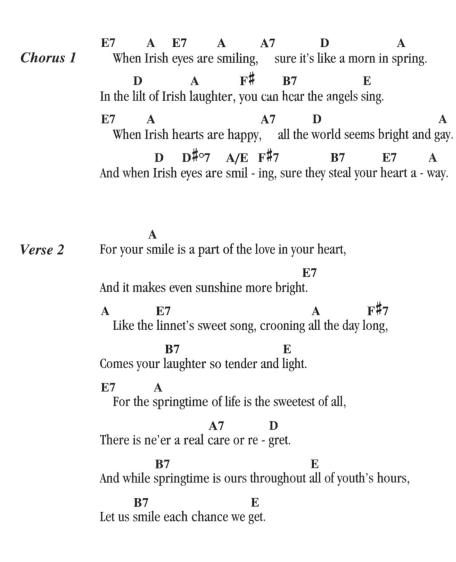

Chorus 1

E7	A	E7	A	A7	D	A

When Irish eyes are smiling,   sure it's like a morn in spring.

D   A   F♯   B7   E

In the lilt of Irish laughter, you can hear the angels sing.

E7   A   A7   D   A

When Irish hearts are happy,   all the world seems bright and gay.

D   D♯°7   A/E   F♯7   B7   E7   A

And when Irish eyes are smil - ing, sure they steal your heart a - way.

Verse 2

A

For your smile is a part of the love in your heart,

E7

And it makes even sunshine more bright.

A   E7   A   F♯7

Like the linnet's sweet song, crooning all the day long,

B7   E

Comes your laughter so tender and light.

E7   A

For the springtime of life is the sweetest of all,

A7   D

There is ne'er a real care or re - gret.

B7   E

And while springtime is ours throughout all of youth's hours,

B7   E

Let us smile each chance we get.

Chorus 2   *Repeat Chorus 1*

Where the River Shannon Flows

By James J. Russell

Melody:

There's a pret - ty spot in Ire - land

Intro

|D F#7 |Bm7 D7 |G |D/F# |

|G Em |F#m Bm7 |Em7 |A7 |

Verse 1

        D   A7   D
There's a pretty spot in Ireland

  G   D
I always claim for my land.

       G   D
Where the fairies and the blarney

    E7   Bb7 A7
Will never, never die.

G/B A/C# D   A7   Bm7
It's the   land of the shil - lalah.

Am7 D7 G   D
      My heart goes back there daily,

     G C G   D
To the girl I left be - hind me

Bm7   Em   A7sus4 A7   D
When we kissed and said   good - bye.

Chorus 1

      G   D
Where dear old Shannon's flowing,

D7   G   D
Where the three-leaved shamrock grows.

         G   D
Where my heart is, I am going,

Bm7   E7   A7
  To my little Irish rose.

         D   F#7/A# Bm7
And the moment that I   meet her,

Am7 D7 G   D
      With a hug and kiss I'll greet her,

       G   Em7   D
For there's not a colleen sweeter

Bm7   Em7 G/A A7 D
Where the River Shan - non flows.

Interlude   *Repeat Intro*

Verse 2

        D   A7   D
Sure no letter I'll be mailing,

   G   D
For soon I will be sailing.

      G   D
And I'll bless the ship that takes me

      E7   Bb7   A7
To my dear old Erin's shore.

G/B A/C# D   A7   Bm7
There I'll   settle down for - ever.

Am7 D7 G   D
    I'll leave my old sod never,

      G   C G   D
And I'll whis - per to my sweetheart,

Bm7   Em   A7sus4 A7 D
"Come and take my name, As - thore."

Chorus 2   *Repeat Chorus 1*

Whiskey in the Jar

Traditional Irish Folk Song

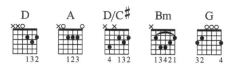

Intro |D   A |D | |

Verse 1

    D   **D/C♯ Bm**
As I was goin' over the Cork and Kerry mountains,

 G   **D** **D/C♯ Bm**
Met with Captain Farrell and his money he was countin'.

  D   **D/C♯ Bm**
I first produced me pistol, then produced me rapier.

   G   **D** **D/C♯ Bm**
Sing, "Stand and deliver. I am the boldest saver."

    A
Musha ring dumma doorama da.

Chorus 1

  D   **D/C♯ A**
 Whack for the daddyo,

Bm   **G**
 Whack for the daddyo.

    D **A** **D**
There's whiskey in the jar.

Verse 2

       D   **D/C♯ Bm**
I counted out his money;   paid a pretty penny.

G   **D**   **D/C♯**   **Bm**
Put it in me pocket and I took it home to Jenny.

       D   **D/C♯ Bm**
And she sighed and she swore,   she never would deceive me.

      G   **D**   **D/C♯ Bm**
The devil take the woman for they never can be easy.

         A
With sha - reem dumma doorama da.

Chorus 2   *Repeat Chorus 1*

Verse 3

       D   **D/C♯ Bm**
It was early in the morning,   be - fore I rose to travel.

G   **D**   **D/C♯ Bm**
Up rides a band of footmen and like - wise rasher Farrell.

       D   **D/C♯ Bm**
Well, I drew upon me pistol,   she stole away me rapier.

G   **D**   **D/C♯ Bm**
Couldn't shoot the water, so a pris'ner I was   taken.

       A
Musha ring dumma doorama da.

Chorus 3   *Repeat Chorus 1*

Verse 4

D D/C♯ Bm
Some take delight in the fishin' and the fowlin',

G D D/C♯ Bm
Others take delight in the carriage gently rollin'.

D D/C♯ Bm
Ah, but I take delight in the juice of the barley.

G D D/C♯ Bm
Courtin' pretty women in the moun - tains of Killar - ney.

A
Musha ring dumma doorama da.

Chorus 4

D D/C♯ A
Whack for the daddyo,

Bm G
Whack for the daddyo.

D A D
There's whiskey in the jar.

A
Musha ring dumma doorama da.

D D/C♯ A
Whack for the daddyo,

Bm G
Whack for the daddyo.

D A D
There's whiskey in the jar.

The Wild Colonial Boy

Australian Folksong

Melody:

There was   a   wild   co - lo - nial

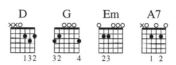

D   G   Em   A7

Intro

|D | |G |Em |
|A7 | |D |A7 |

Verse 1

　　　　　　A7　　　　　G　　Em　　A7　　　　　　　D
There was a wild co - lonial boy, Jack Duggan was his name.

　　　　　　　　　　　　　A7　　　　　G　　　　A7　　D
He was born and raised in Ireland in a place called Castle - main.

　　　　　　　　　　　A7　　　　G　　　A7　　　D
He was his father's only son, his mother's pride and joy,

　　　　　　　　　　G　　　Em　　A7　　　　　D　A7
And dearly did his parents love the wild colonial boy.

Verse 2

　　　　　　A7　　　　G　　Em　　　A7　　　　　　D
At the early age of sixteen years, he left his native home,

　　　　　　　　　　　　　A7　　　　　G　　　A7　　　D
And through Australia's sunny clime he was in - clined to roam.

　　　　　　　　　　　A7　　　　G　　　A7　　　D
He robbed the lordly squatters, their flocks he would de - stroy,

　　　　　　　　G　　Em　　A7　　　　D　A7
A terror to Aus - tralia was the wild colonial boy.

Verse 3

     A7   G   Em   A7   D
For two long years this darling youth ran on his wild ca - reer,

                       A7   G   A7   D
With a heart that knew no danger, their justice did not fear.

                A7   G   A7   D
He stuck the Beechworth coach up, and he robbed Judge Mc - E - voy,

               G   Em A7   D A7
Who trembling gave his gold up to the wild colonial boy.

Verse 4

     A7   G   Em   A7   D
He bade the judge "Good morning" and he told him to be - ware,

                 A7   G   A7   D
For he never robbed an honest judge what acted "on the square."

            A7   G   A7 D
Yet you would rob a mother of her son and only joy,

            G   Em   A7   D A7
And breed a race of outlaws like the wild colonial boy.

Verse 5

     A7   G   Em   A7   D
One morning on the prairie Wild Jack Duggan rode a - long,

               A7   G   A7   D
While listening to the mockingbirds sing - ing a cheerful song.

              A7   G   A7   D
Out jumped three troopers fierce and grim, Kelly, Davis and Fitz - Roy,

            G   Em   A7   D A7
They all set out to capture him, the wild colonial boy.

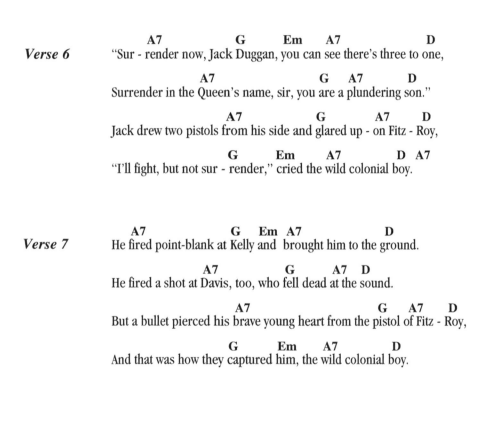

Verse 6

　　　　　　　　　A7　　　　　　　　G　　　Em　　A7　　　　　　　　　　D
"Sur - render now, Jack Duggan, you can see there's three to one,

　　　　　　　　　　A7　　　　　　　　　　G　　A7　　　D
Surrender in the Queen's name, sir, you are a plundering son."

　　　　　　　　　　A7　　　　　　　G　　　　A7　　　D
Jack drew two pistols from his side and glared up - on Fitz - Roy,

　　　　　　　　　G　　　Em　　　A7　　　　　D　A7
"I'll fight, but not sur - render," cried the wild colonial boy.

Verse 7

　　　　　　　A7　　　　　　　G　　Em　A7　　　　　D
He fired point-blank at Kelly and　brought him to the ground.

　　　　　　　　A7　　　　　G　　　A7　D
He fired a shot at Davis, too, who fell dead at the sound.

　　　　　　　　　A7　　　　　　　　　　G　　A7　　　D
But a bullet pierced his brave young heart from the pistol of Fitz - Roy,

　　　　　　　　G　　　Em　　　A7　　　　　D
And that was how they captured him, the wild colonial boy.

Whiskey, You're the Devil

Traditional Irish Folksong

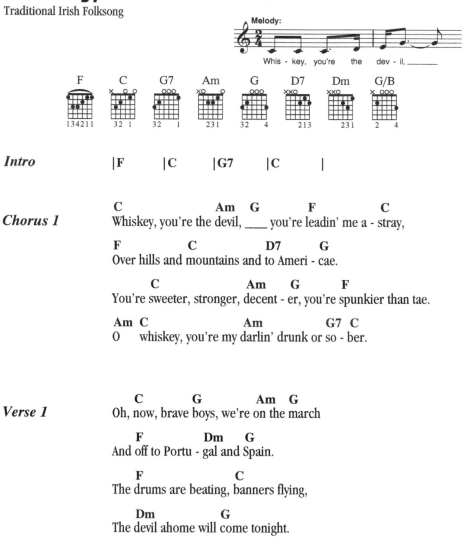

Intro

|F |C |G7 |C |

Chorus 1

C   Am   G   F   C
Whiskey, you're the devil, ___ you're leadin' me a - stray,

F   C   D7   G
Over hills and mountains and to Ameri - cae.

      C   Am   G   F
You're sweeter, stronger, decent - er, you're spunkier than tae.

Am C   Am   G7 C
O   whiskey, you're my darlin' drunk or so - ber.

Verse 1

      C   G   Am   G
Oh, now, brave boys, we're on the march

      F   Dm   G
And off to Portu - gal and Spain.

      F   C
The drums are beating, banners flying,

      Dm   G
The devil ahome will come tonight.

C   G   C
Love, fare thee well with me tithery eye, the doodelum, the da,

      G7   F
Me tithery eye, the doodelum, the da,

G/B Am   C   F   G   C
  Me rikes fall, tour a laddie, oh, there's whiskey in the jar!

Copyright © 2009 by HAL LEONARD CORPORATION
International Copyright Secured All Rights Reserved

GUITAR CHORD SONGBOOK

Chorus 2   *Repeat Chorus 1*

Verse 2
     C   G Am G F   Dm G
     The French are fighting bold - ly, men dying hot and cold - ly.

      F   C   Dm   G
     Gives ev'ry man his flask of powder, his farlock on his shoulder.

    C G   C
    Love, fare thee well with me tithery eye, the doodelum, the da,

    G7   F
    Me tithery eye, the doodelum, the da,

    G/B Am   C   F   G C
     Me rikes fall, tour a laddie, oh, there's whiskey in the jar!

Chorus 3   *Repeat Chorus 1*

Verse 3
      C   G Am G
     Said the mother, "So not wrong me;

      F   Dm G
     Don't take my daughter from me.

      F   C
     For if you do, I will torment you,

      Dm   G
     And after death a ghost will haunt you."

    C G   C
    Love, fare thee well with me tithery eye, the doodelum, the da,

    G7   F
    Me tithery eye, the doodelum, the da,

    G/B Am   C   F   G C
     Me rikes fall, tour a laddie, oh, there's whiskey in the jar!

Chorus 4   *Repeat Chorus 1*

Wild Rover

Traditional Irish Folk Song

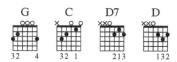

Intro

|G | | |C |
|G |D7 |G | |

Verse 1

        G   **C**
I've been a wild rover for many a year,

         G   **D7**   **G**
And I've spent all my money on whiskey and beer.

                           C
But now I'm returning with gold in great store,

        G   **D7**   **G**
And I never will play the wild rover no more.

Chorus 1

        D   **G**   **C**
And it's no, nay, never;   no, nay, never no more

      G   **C**   **G**   **D7** **G**
Will I play the wild rover, no, never ____ no more.

Verse 2

              G   C
I went into an ale house I used to fre - quent,

              G   D7   G
And I told the land - lady my money was spent.

                                  C
I asked for a bottle, she answered me, "Nay,

             G   D7   G
Such a custom as yours I can get any day."

Chorus 2   *Repeat Chorus 1*

Verse 3

              G   C
Then out of my pocket, I took sov'reigns bright,

             G   D7   G
And the landlady's eyes opened wide with de - light.

                                 C
She said, "I have whiskeys and wines of the best,

             G   D7   G
And the words that I said, sure, were only in jest."

Chorus 3   *Repeat Chorus 1*

Verse 4

              G   C
I'll go back to my parents, confess what I've done,

             G   D7   G
And ask them to pardon their prodigal son.

                               C
And if they caress me as ofttimes be - fore,

             G   D7   G
Then I never will play the wild rover no more.

Chorus 4   *Repeat Chorus 1*

Guitar Chord Songbooks

Each book includes complete lyrics, chord symbols, and guitar chord diagrams.

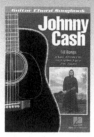 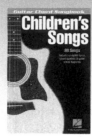  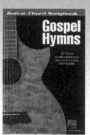 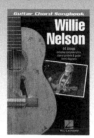

Acoustic Hits
More than 60 songs: Against the Wind • Name • One • Southern Cross • Take Me Home, Country Roads • Teardrops on My Guitar • Who'll Stop the Rain • Ziggy Stardust • and more.
00701787 ....$14.99

Acoustic Rock
80 acoustic favorites: Blackbird • Blowin' in the Wind • Layla • Maggie May • Me and Julio down by the Schoolyard • Pink Houses • and more.
00699540................................$21.99

Alabama
50 of Alabama's best: Angels Among Us • The Closer You Get • If You're Gonna Play in Texas (You Gotta Have a Fiddle in the Band) • Mountain Music • When We Make Love • and more.
00699914................................$14.95

The Beach Boys
59 favorites: California Girls • Don't Worry Baby • Fun, Fun, Fun • Good Vibrations • Help Me Rhonda • Wouldn't It Be Nice • dozens more!
00699566................................$19.99

The Beatles
100 more Beatles hits: Lady Madonna • Let It Be • Ob-La-Di, Ob-La-Da • Paperback Writer • Revolution • Twist and Shout • When I'm Sixty-Four • and more.
00699562................................$17.99

Bluegrass
Over 40 classics: Blue Moon of Kentucky • Foggy Mountain Top • High on a Mountain Top • Keep on the Sunny Side • Wabash Cannonball • The Wreck of the Old '97 • and more.
00702585................................$14.99

Johnny Cash
58 Cash classics: A Boy Named Sue • Cry, Cry, Cry • Daddy Sang Bass • Folsom Prison Blues • I Walk the Line • RIng of Fire • Solitary Man • and more.
00699648................................$17.99

Children's Songs
70 songs for kids: Alphabet Song • Bingo • The Candy Man • Eensy Weensy Spider • Puff the Magic Dragon • Twinkle, Twinkle Little Star • and more.
00699539................................$16.99

Christmas Carols
80 Christmas carols: Angels We Have Heard on High • The Holly and the Ivy • I Saw Three Ships • Joy to the World • O Holy Night • and more.
00699536................................$12.99

Christmas Songs
80 songs: All I Want for Christmas Is My Two Front Teeth • Baby, It's Cold Outside • Jingle Bell Rock • Mistletoe and Holly • Sleigh Ride • and more.
00119911................................$14.99

Eric Clapton
75 of Slowhand's finest: I Shot the Sheriff • Knockin' on Heaven's Door • Layla • Strange Brew • Tears in Heaven • Wonderful Tonight • and more.
00699567 ....$19.99

Classic Rock
80 rock essentials: Beast of Burden • Cat Scratch Fever • Hot Blooded • Money • Rhiannon • Sweet Emotion • Walk on the Wild Side • and more.
00699598 ....$18.99

Coffeehouse Hits
57 singer-songwriter hits: Don't Know Why • Hallelujah • Meet Virginia • Steal My Kisses • Torn • Wonderwall • You Learn • and more.
00703318 ....$14.99

Country
80 country standards: Boot Scootin' Boogie • Crazy • Hey, Good Lookin' • Sixteen Tons • Through the Years • Your Cheatin' Heart • and more.
00699534 ....$17.99

Country Favorites
Over 60 songs: Achy Breaky Heart (Don't Tell My Heart) • Brand New Man • Gone Country • The Long Black Veil • Make the World Go Away • and more.
00700609 ....$14.99

Country Hits
40 classics: As Good As I Once Was • Before He Cheats • Cruise • Follow Your Arrow • God Gave Me You • The House That Built Me • Just a Kiss • Making Memories of Us • Need You Now • Your Man • and more.
00140859 ....$14.99

Country Standards
60 songs: By the Time I Get to Phoenix • El Paso • The Gambler • I Fall to Pieces • Jolene • King of the Road • Put Your Hand in the Hand • A Rainy Night in Georgia • and more.
00700608 ....$12.95

Cowboy Songs
Over 60 tunes: Back in the Saddle Again • Happy Trails • Home on the Range • Streets of Laredo • The Yellow Rose of Texas • and more.
00699636 ....$19.99

Creedence Clearwater Revival
34 CCR classics: Bad Moon Rising • Born on the Bayou • Down on the Corner • Fortunate Son • Up Around the Bend • and more.
00701786 ....$16.99

Jim Croce
37 tunes: Bad, Bad Leroy Brown • I Got a Name • I'll Have to Say I Love You in a Song • Operator (That's Not the Way It Feels) • Photographs and Memories • Time in a Bottle • You Don't Mess Around with Jim • and many more.
00148087 ....$14.99

Crosby, Stills & Nash
37 hits: Chicago • Dark Star • Deja Vu • Marrakesh Express • Our House • Southern Cross • Suite: Judy Blue Eyes • Teach Your Children • and more.
00701609.................................$16.99

John Denver
50 favorites: Annie's Song • Leaving on a Jet Plane • Rocky Mountain High • Take Me Home, Country Roads • Thank God I'm a Country Boy • and more.
02501697.................................$17.99

Neil Diamond
50 songs: America • Cherry, Cherry • Cracklin' Rosie • Forever in Blue Jeans • I Am...I Said • Love on the Rocks • Song Sung Blue • Sweet Caroline • and dozens more!
00700606 ....$19.99

Disney
56 super Disney songs: Be Our Guest • Friend like Me • Hakuna Matata • It's a Small World • Under the Sea • A Whole New World • Zip-A-Dee-Doo-Dah • and more.
00701071 ....$17.99

The Doors
60 classics from the Doors: Break on Through to the Other Side • Hello, I Love You (Won't You Tell Me Your Name?) • Light My Fire • Love Her Madly • Riders on the Storm • Touch Me • and more.
00699888 ....$17.99

Eagles
40 familiar songs: Already Gone • Best of My Love • Desperado • Hotel California • Life in the Fast Lane • Peaceful Easy Feeling • Witchy Woman • more.
00122917 ....$16.99

Early Rock
80 classics: All I Have to Do Is Dream • Big Girls Don't Cry • Fever • Itsy Bitsy Teenie Weenie Yellow Polkadot Bikini • Let's Twist Again • Lollipop • and more.
00699916 ....$14.99

Folk Pop Rock
80 songs: American Pie • Dust in the Wind • Me and Bobby McGee • Somebody to Love • Time in a Bottle • and more.
00699651 ....$17.99

Folksongs
80 folk favorites: Aura Lee • Camptown Races • Danny Boy • Man of Constant Sorrow • Nobody Knows the Trouble I've Seen • and more.
00699541 ....$14.99

40 Easy Strumming Songs
Features 40 songs: Cat's in the Cradle • Daughter • Hey, Soul Sister • Homeward Bound • Take It Easy • Wild Horses • and more.
00115972 ....$16.99

Four Chord Songs
40 hit songs: Blowin' in the Wind • I Saw Her Standing There • Should I Stay or Should I Go • Stand by Me • Turn the Page • Wonderful Tonight • and more.
00701611 ....$14.99

Glee
50+ hits: Bad Romance • Beautiful • Dancing with Myself • Don't Stop Believin' • Imagine • Rehab • Teenage Dream • True Colors • and dozens more.
00702501 ....$14.99

Gospel Hymns
80 hymns: Amazing Grace • Give Me That Old Time Religion • I Love to Tell the Story • Shall We Gather at the River? • Wondrous Love • and more.
00700463 ....$14.99

Grand Ole Opry®
80 great songs: Abilene • Act Naturally • Country Boy • Crazy • Friends in Low Places • He Stopped Loving Her Today • Wings of a Dove • dozens more!
00699885 ....$16.95

Grateful Dead
30 favorites: Casey Jones • Friend of the Devil • High Time • Ramble on Rose • Ripple • Rosemary • Sugar Magnolia • Truckin' • Uncle John's Band • more.
00139461 ....$14.99

Green Day
34 faves: American Idiot • Basket Case • Boulevard of Broken Dreams • Good Riddance (Time of Your Life) • 21 Guns • Wake Me Up When September Ends • When I Come Around • and more.
00103074 ....$14.99

Irish Songs
45 Irish favorites: Danny Boy • Girl I Left Behind Me • Harrigan • I'll Tell Me Ma • The Irish Rover • My Wild Irish Rose • When Irish Eyes Are Smiling • and more!
00701044 ....$14.99

Michael Jackson
27 songs: Bad • Beat It • Billie Jean • Black or White (Rap Version) • Don't Stop 'Til You Get Enough • The Girl Is Mine • Man in the Mirror • Rock with You • Smooth Criminal • Thriller • more.
00137847 ....$14.99

Billy Joel
60 Billy Joel favorites: • It's Still Rock and Roll to Me • The Longest Time • Piano Man • She's Always a Woman • Uptown Girl • We Didn't Start the Fire • You May Be Right • and more.
00699632 ....$19.99

Elton John
60 songs: Bennie and the Jets • Candle in the Wind • Crocodile Rock • Goodbye Yellow Brick Road • Sad Songs Say So Much • Tiny Dancer • Your Song • more.
00699732 ....$15.99

Ray LaMontagne
20 songs: Empty • Gossip in the Grain • Hold You in My Arms • I Still Care for You • Jolene • Trouble • You Are the Best Thing • and more.
00130337.................................$12.99

Latin Songs
60 favorites: Bésame Mucho (Kiss Me Much) • The Girl from Ipanema (Garôta De Ipanema) • The Look of Love • So Nice (Summer Samba) • and more.
00700973 ....$14.99

Love Songs
65 romantic ditties: Baby, I'm-A Want You • Fields of Gold • Here, There and Everywhere • Let's Stay Together • Never My Love • The Way We Were • more!
00701043.................................$14.99

Bob Marley
36 songs: Buffalo Soldier • Get up Stand Up • I Shot the Sheriff • Is This Love • No Woman No Cry • One Love • Redemption Song • and more.
00701704.................................$17.99

Bruno Mars
15 hits: Count on Me • Grenade • If I Knew • Just the Way You Are • The Lazy Song • Locked Out of Heaven • Marry You • Treasure • When I Was Your Man • and more.
00125332 ....$12.99

Paul McCartney
60 from Sir Paul: Band on the Run • Jet • Let 'Em In • Maybe I'm Amazed • No More Lonely Nights • Say Say Say • Take It Away • With a Little Luck • and more!
00385035 ....$16.95

Steve Miller
33 hits: Dance Dance Dance • Jet Airliner • The Joker • Jungle Love • Rock'n Me • Serenade from the Stars • Swingtown • Take the Money and Run • and more.
00701146.................................$12.99

Modern Worship
80 modern worship favorites: All Because of Jesus • Amazed • Everlasting God • Happy Day • I Am Free • Jesus Messiah • and more.
00701801 ....$16.99

Motown
60 Motown masterpieces: ABC • Baby I Need Your Lovin' • I'll Be There • Stop! In the Name of Love • You Can't Hurry Love • and more.
00699734 ....$17.99

Willie Nelson
44 favorites: Always on My Mind • Beer for My Horses • Blue Skies • Georgia on My Mind • Help Me Make It Through the Night • On the Road Again • Whiskey River • and many more.
00148273 ....$17.99

Nirvana
40 songs: About a Girl • Come as You Are • Heart Shaped Box • The Man Who Sold the World • Smells like Teen Spirit • You Know You're Right • and more.
00699762 ....$16.99

Roy Orbison
38 songs: Blue Bayou • Oh, Pretty Woman • Only the Lonely (Know the Way I Feel) • Working for the Man • You Got It • and more.
00699752 ....$17.99

Peter, Paul & Mary
43 favorites: If I Had a Hammer (The Hammer Song) • Leaving on a Jet Plane • Puff the Magic Dragon • This Land Is Your Land • and more.
00103013................................$19.99

Tom Petty
American Girl • Breakdown • Don't Do Me like That • Free Fallin' • Here Comes My Girl • Into the Great Wide Open • Mary Jane's Last Dance • Refugee • Runnin' Down a Dream • The Waiting • and more.
00699883 ....$15.99

Pink Floyd
30 songs: Another Brick in the Wall, Part 2 • Brain Damage • Breathe • Comfortably Numb • Hey You • Money • Mother • Run like Hell • Us and Them • Wish You Were Here • Young Lust • and many more.
00139116 ....$14.99

Pop/Rock
80 chart hits: Against All Odds • Come Sail Away • Every Breath You Take • Hurts So Good • Kokomo • More Than Words • Smooth • Summer of '69 • and more.
00699538 ....$16.99

Praise and Worship
80 favorites: Agnus Dei • He Is Exalted • I Could Sing of Your Love Forever • Lord, I Lift Your Name on High • More Precious Than Silver • Open the Eyes of My Heart • Shine, Jesus, Shine • and more.
00699634 ....$14.99

Elvis Presley
60 hits: All Shook Up • Blue Suede Shoes • Can't Help Falling in Love • Heartbreak Hotel • Hound Dog • Jailhouse Rock • Suspicious Minds • Viva Las Vegas • and more.
00699633 ....$17.99

Queen
40 hits: Bohemian Rhapsody • Crazy Little Thing Called Love • Fat Bottomed Girls • Killer Queen • Tie Your Mother Down • Under Pressure • You're My Best Friend • and more!
00702395 ....$14.99

Red Hot Chili Peppers
50 hits: Californication • Give It Away • Higher Ground • Love Rollercoaster • Scar Tissue • Suck My Kiss • Under the Bridge • and more.
00699710 ....$19.99

The Rolling Stones
35 hits: Angie • Beast of Burden • Fool to Cry • Happy • It's Only Rock 'N' Roll (But I Like It) • Miss You • Not Fade Away • Respectable • Rocks Off • Start Me Up • Time Is on My Side • Tumbling Dice • Waiting on a Friend • and more.
00137716 ....$17.99

Bob Seger
41 favorites: Against the Wind • Hollywood Nights • Katmandu • Like a Rock • Night Moves • Old Time Rock & Roll • You'll Accomp'ny Me • and more!
00701147................................$12.99

Carly Simon
Nearly 40 classic hits, including: Anticipation • Haven't Got Time for the Pain • Jesse • Let the River Run • Nobody Does It Better • You're So Vain • and more.
00121011................................$14.99

Sting
50 favorites from Sting and the Police: Don't Stand So Close to Me • Every Breath You Take • Fields of Gold • King of Pain • Message in a Bottle • Roxanne • and more.
00699921 ....$17.99

Taylor Swift
40 tunes: Back to December • Bad Blood • Blank Space • Fearless • Fifteen • I Knew You Were Trouble • Look What You Made Me Do • Love Story • Mean • Shake It Off • Speak Now • Wildest Dreams • and many more.
00263755................................$16.99

Three Chord Acoustic Songs
30 acoustic songs: All Apologies • Blowin' in the Wind • Hold My Hand • Just the Way You Are • Ring of Fire • Shelter from the Storm • This Land Is Your Land • and more.
00123860 ....$14.99

Three Chord Songs
65 includes: All Right Now • La Bamba • Lay Down Sally • Mony, Mony • Rock Around the Clock • Rock This Town • Werewolves of London • You Are My Sunshine • and more.
00699720 ....$17.99

Two-Chord Songs
Nearly 60 songs: ABC • Brick House • Eleanor Rigby • Fever • Paperback Writer • Ramblin' Man Tulsa Time • When Love Comes to Town • and more.
00119236................................$16.99

U2
40 U2 songs: Beautiful Day • Mysterious Ways • New Year's Day • One • Sunday Bloody Sunday • Walk On • Where the Streets Have No Name • With or Without You • and more.
00137744................................$14.99

Hank Williams
68 classics: Cold, Cold Heart • Hey, Good Lookin' • Honky Tonk Blues • I'm a Long Gone Daddy • Jambalaya (On the Bayou) • Your Cheatin' Heart • and more.
00700607 ....$16.99

Stevie Wonder
40 of Stevie's best: For Once in My Life • Higher Ground • Isn't She Lovely • My Cherie Amour • Sir Duke • Superstition • Uptight (Everything's Alright) • Yester-Me, Yester-You, Yesterday • and more!
00120862 ....$14.99

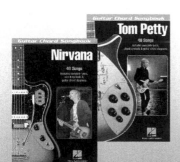

HAL•LEONARD®

Prices, contents and availability subject to change without notice.

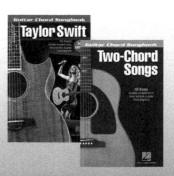